Teaching English in Rural Communities

Teaching English in Rural Communities

Toward a Critical Rural English Pedagogy

Robert Petrone
Allison Wynhoff Olsen

ROWMAN & LITTLEFIELD
Lanham • Boulder • New York • London

Published by Rowman & Littlefield
An imprint of The Rowman & Littlefield Publishing Group, Inc.
4501 Forbes Boulevard, Suite 200, Lanham, Maryland 20706
www.rowman.com

6 Tinworth Street, London, SE11 5AL, United Kingdom

Copyright © 2021 by Robert Petrone & Allison Wynhoff Olsen

All rights reserved. No part of this book may be reproduced in any form or by any electronic or mechanical means, including information storage and retrieval systems, without written permission from the publisher, except by a reviewer who may quote passages in a review.

British Library Cataloguing in Publication Information Available

Library of Congress Cataloging-in-Publication Data

Names: Petrone, Robert, 1974– author. | Wynhoff Olsen, Allison, 1976– author.
Title: Teaching English in rural communities : toward a critical rural English pedagogy / Robert Petrone, Allison Wynhoff Olsen.
Description: Lanham : Rowman & Littlefield, [2021] | Includes bibliographical references and index. | Summary: "Drawing upon classroom practices, Teaching English in Rural Communities articulates and develops a Critical Rural English Pedagogy."—Provided by publisher.
Identifiers: LCCN 2020048971 (print) | LCCN 2020048972 (ebook) | ISBN 9781475849165 (cloth) | ISBN 9781475849172 (paperback) | ISBN 9781475849189 (epub)
Subjects: LCSH: English language—Study and teaching (Secondary)—United States. | English language—Study and teaching (Elementary)—United States. | Education, Rural—United States.
Classification: LCC LB1631 .P448 2021 (print) | LCC LB1631 (ebook) | DDC 428.0071/2—dc23
LC record available at https://lccn.loc.gov/2020048971
LC ebook record available at https://lccn.loc.gov/2020048972

Contents

Foreword by Dr. Valerie Kinloch   vii

Preface   xi

Acknowledgments   xv

PART I: WHY A CRITICAL RURAL ENGLISH PEDAGOGY?   1

1   Moving Toward a Critical Rural English Pedagogy   3
Robert Petrone and Allison Wynhoff Olsen

PART II: INSIDE RURAL ENGLISH CLASSROOMS   13

2   We Ain't Much to Look At: Teaching about Rurality through Literary Texts   15
Alli Behrens, Robert Petrone, and Allison Wynhoff Olsen

3   Who Has a "Place" in Place-Based Pedagogy?: Indigenizing Rural English Education   39
Melissa Horner, Robert Petrone, and Allison Wynhoff Olsen

4   Linking Local Communities to Critical Rural English Pedagogies   73
Robert Petrone, Allison Wynhoff Olsen, Elizabeth Reierson, and Catherine Dorian

PART III: MOVING FORWARD   99

5   Re-Thinking Race/ism and Rurality in English Education   101
Melissa Horner, Robert Petrone, and Allison Wynhoff Olsen

6	Opportunities and Challenges in Moving Toward a Critical Rural English Pedagogy *Robert Petrone and Allison Wynhoff Olsen*	119

Appendix A: Assignment Sheet for Textbook Entry Project   137

Appendix B: Student Sample   141

References   145

Index   155

About the Authors   161

Foreword

TOWARD A CRITICAL RURAL ENGLISH PEDAGOGY

Critical Rural English Pedagogy [is a] framework for developing and implementing English curricula that centers rurality as an analytic focus for critical literacy practices . . . [it] both addresses the local *and* broader discursive constructions of rurality. (Petrone & Wynhoff Olsen, Chapter 1)

Teaching English in Rural Communities: Toward a Critical Rural English Pedagogy is a beautifully constructed book that examines meanings of engagement and place-based pedagogies by inviting students, teachers, and teacher educators to grapple with questions of power and representations of rurality within and beyond the curriculum. From the very beginning to the end of this book, authors Robert Petrone and Allison Wynhoff Olsen ask readers to consider the following larger questions that frame their teaching and research on Critical Rural English Pedagogy (CREP): "What is it like to be an English teacher in a rural and remote community? What are the unique challenges and opportunities for learning and teaching English in these contexts? How can English teachers best be prepared and/or supported to work in these rural and remote schools?" And, thus, begins the important journey of Petrone and Wynhoff Olsen to situate as central the stories "of triumph and tears, isolation and celebration, burnout and beauty" of many English teachers working within rural schools. In fact, their journey advocates for new, inclusive, and humanizing ways by which we all should see, hear, and affirm the lives and literacies of children, youth, families, friends, teachers, and community members who reside and work in rural contexts.

If, as the authors argue, the power of CREP lies with its ability to facilitate students' engagements with texts—from how students design texts, produce texts as counternarratives to negative depictions of rurality, create texts that disrupt images of rurality as isolated, isolating, and violent—then its deeper relevance lies with its ability to transform English Education into a site of critical place-based engagements *with* the curriculum and *within* the world. Doing so necessarily nuances and complicates understandings of rurality. This is especially the case when the focus is placed on how classroom teachers within rural educational contexts not only create curricula as well as teach and learn with students but also serve as class sponsors, debate advisors, mentors, sports coaches, game referees, and, among other roles, neighbors.

In the book's three parts—"Why a Critical Rural English Pedagogy?" (part I), "Inside Rural English Classrooms" (part II), and "Moving Forward" (part III)—readers are introduced to connections among social justice, equity, and CREP. We meet Alli Behrens, a teacher working in the community of Whitehall, which is in the southwestern part of Montana. She takes up connections among justice, equity, and CREP through curricular engagements focused on rurality within literature and media texts. We also meet Melissa Horner, a teacher working in Park City, which is in the south-central part of Montana, and working within a predominately white rural school. She created a curriculum centered on Native American authors and texts and focused on deeply exploring topics of land, tribal sovereignty, and anti-colonialism within the #NODAPL movement. Then, we are introduced to Liz Reierson, a teacher working in Miles City, which is in close proximity to the Yellowstone River. She works with students to examine connections as well as dissonances among poetry, place, and the various literacies within their local community. Finally, we are introduced to Catherine Dorian, a teacher working in Fort Benton, which resides on the ancestral homelands of the Piikani (Blackfeet) Tribal Nation. She developed curriculum that examines the intersections of rurality, reputation, sexuality, and race. Alli Behrens, Melissa Horner, Liz Reierson, and Catherine Dorian are but four of many other teachers who understand CREP as a framing by which to investigate meanings and representations of rural and rurality within the curriculum. They also realize the valuable role of CREP in relation to how teachers can encourage students (and be encouraged themselves) to question, interrogate, resist, and produce counternarratives to the many negative portrayals and representations of "rural" that get enacted onto lives and lands, and within teaching and learning. Such ways of being can, I believe, contribute to more expansive views of teaching and learning, generally, and English Education and literacy teaching and learning, specifically, that are grounded in relevant, responsive, and humanizing practices for students and teachers, for families and communities, and for education theory and practice.

It is my hope that as we read this book, we all will begin to (re)imagine and (re)create classrooms as lovingly critical spaces. That we will remain open to engaging in deep explorations into differences and diversities, on the one hand, and examinations into how classrooms and curricula can lead to educational equity, on the other hand. *Because* of how and why we teach. *Because* of how and why we disrupt negative depictions of places and people. *Because* of how and why we encourage students, as they encourage us, to see the world in relation to and also beyond the realities of our own classrooms. *Because* of how and why we must talk openly about and work for justice, equity, and intersectionality in our teaching and research. *Because* of how and why we must be more responsive to creating and sustaining a more equitable world that includes nuanced, critical, and humanizing readings and renderings of rurality. *Because* we must.

Thank you, Robert Petrone and Allison Wynhoff Olsen, for adding needed perspectives into this discussion. Thank you for providing us with a text that not only contributes to the literature on rural education but also reminds us to always see teachers, students, and families within and beyond rural communities as part of our democratic project for equitable and just schooling.

Valerie Kinloch (vkinloch@pitt.edu)
Renée and Richard Goldman Endowed Dean and Professor
School of Education at the University of Pittsburgh
NCTE Presidential Team, 2019–2023

Preface

This book was born out of a long-term collaboration between the two of us during our shared time as English Education faculty members at Montana State University (MSU). Given the combination of Montana's vastness as the 4th largest state and its low population density (ranked 3rd lowest only behind neighboring Wyoming and Alaska), we designed our English teacher education program to prepare and support secondary English teachers for the unique challenges and opportunities inherent within rural schools—the contexts most of our undergraduates entered as they began their careers.

Throughout our shared time at MSU, we drove across Montana to meet with English teachers, visit their schools, spend time in their communities, and, as best as we could, understand the day-to-day realities (or, as we have come to think of them, *rura*lities) of their lives in and out of work. The central questions driving our research were the following: What is it like to be an English teacher in a rural and remote community? What are the unique challenges and opportunities for learning and teaching English in these contexts? How can English teachers best be prepared and/or supported to work in these rural and remote schools?

For Allison, this work was a sort of homecoming, as her nine years of high school teaching were in small rural schools in Minnesota. Her interests in rural English Education emerged from these earliest, formative experiences, particularly as she and her rural students achieved successes and learning gains that disproved theories and "best practices" but centered relationships. She felt that neither her preparation for teaching nor the support she received along the way spoke directly to her rural teaching experiences. Thus, a big part of her leaving the classroom to get a doctorate and become a teacher educator and educational researcher was to help examine the experiences of rural English teachers and the best ways to support them.

For Robert, the attention to rurality was new upon arriving to Montana State University. Having grown up and been a teacher in and near major cities (i.e., New York City, Denver), Robert's preparation and interests in teaching high school English always focused on urban schools and issues. It was not until he moved to Montana, where it is virtually impossible to find any space that might reasonably be designated "urban" in comparison to his previous experiences, that issues of rurality came into focus for him. As part of this process, Robert had to grapple with unconscious biases he did not even know he had regarding rurality as a result of his own metro-centricism.

Together, the two of us—one, a rural "insider," and the other an "outsider" to rural—came to this work with a genuine curiosity and openness about what it means—and looks and feels like—to be a secondary English teacher in rural and/or remote schools. Over time, as we sat with dozens and dozens of rural English teachers—in their classrooms, their homes, their local bars—we listened to story after story of triumph and tears, isolation and celebration, burnout and beauty. And the more we learned about and from these rural teachers, the more our curiosity about learning and teaching English in rural communities was piqued. As we have presented about these ideas at national conferences and met rural teachers across the U.S., we have come to understand that the experiences of the teachers we came to know in Montana resonated deeply with rural teachers in other states.

Going into our research, we knew that teaching English in a rural context was a tough job, and the depth of complexity inherent in it quickly made itself apparent. In fact, when we began our research on rural English teaching, we thought we would be talking with teachers mostly about concrete curricular issues; it didn't take long, though, for us to realize that any discussions of curricular resources had to start with understanding the complex ecologies of rural communities and classrooms—as well as the unique place of the English teacher therein. What became readily apparent to us in our research was that teaching secondary English in rural and remote areas is an extremely demanding job—one laden with not just traditional work demands unique to rural teaching but also often taxing psycho-emotional demands as well.

In many rural and remote communities, the job of a secondary English teacher extends well beyond creating curriculum and enacting classroom instruction. As one teacher we interviewed said, the job of the high school English teacher in rural schools is best characterized as "wearing many hats." So, in addition to the normal teaching load (which often includes five or six different preps), English teachers are class sponsors, speech/debate advisors, Future Farmers of America (FFA) mentors, and sports coaches (and when they are not, they are probably calling the games or taking tickets or running concessions), as well as taking on myriad other non-teaching duties.

Unlike many of their suburban and urban counterparts, though, these "extras" are often not options for rural teachers; rather, they are mandated aspects of teaching and generally extend nearly every work day well into evenings when grading papers and preparing for the next day often happen to the point of exhaustion. Virtually every teacher we interviewed over the years talked not only about these multiple demands but also the overt and implicit pressure to be involved in these activities. There was a constant refrain of, as one teacher we interviewed put it: "If I didn't do it, who would? It wouldn't get done, and the kids would miss out."

Furthermore, most teachers in rural and remote contexts live within the community where they teach due to geographic isolation. While there are many benefits to these living arrangements, nearly all of the teachers with whom we have worked also revealed the costs. Specifically, they explained how their lives were always on display and how they would often drive miles out of town in order to shop for more personal items such as tampons and alcohol for fear of running into students or parents—or really anyone from the community—and have gossip spread about them.

One teacher even reported that students, on Monday mornings if she had guests visit over the weekends, would ask her about different cars in her driveway, wanting to know who was visiting her. For this teacher (and many others), she felt there were, at best, blurry boundaries between her work life and her home and personal life—and that she had very little choice in the matter due to the job and living situation.

This personal lack of privacy and anonymity, while similar for most rural teachers, becomes compounded for English teachers since the very nature of the discipline—namely reading and discussing literary texts and writing—often evokes personal connections, affective dimensions to learning, and deeper, more nuanced understandings of students' lives. Teachers we interviewed explained how they cared deeply about their students but felt they knew *too much* sometimes about their students and families, that they themselves felt *too* involved in the community, and that they lacked personal and professional support to manage their knowledge and strain, particularly given the geographic isolation and lack of access to resources like counseling.

In a telling case, one teacher who had worked in a major urban school district for over a decade before moving to and teaching in a small rural community, explained how teaching in an urban district for a decade did not burn her out like fewer than two years in a rural school did because of the intersections of the personal and professional.

As we accumulated story after story of rural English teachers across Montana, we began to conceptualize this book, as we felt it essential that rural English teachers' experiences and stories be disseminated more broadly with the (English) education community. In this way, *Teaching English in Rural*

Communities is both inspired by and written for the teachers we met, talked with, and learned from along the way—the ones who shared their stories with us, who opened up their schools and classrooms to us, and who have inspired us to dig deeper and care more about rural communities, rural schools, rural teachers, and, of course, rural students.

We also write this book as a way to amplify the experiences of rural English teachers for their colleagues who teach in urban and suburban contexts, in an attempt to display some of the exceptional work being done in rural schools and to provide accurate portrayals of what it means to live and teach English in rural and remote communities. Finally, this book is also written for the thousands of practicing and aspiring secondary English teachers who work or hope to work in rural and remote schools throughout the United States—and beyond. Our hats are off to you, and we hope this book will be useful for your work.

Acknowledgments

As this project developed from our shared experiences at Montana State University (MSU), we owe a great deal of gratitude to our colleagues, administration, and support staff at MSU. For this project, we received funding from Montana State's Scholarship & Creativity Grant Program. This seed money enabled us to coordinate a pilot study whereby we visited several teachers throughout Montana and first learned in a concrete way about their experiences.

This initial experience was pivotal for our work, and without the support we received to make it happen, this project would have likely never developed and this book never written. Building upon this pilot data, we also received a Small Research Grant from the Spencer Foundation, which enabled us to scale up our research. We are indebted to the Spencer Foundation's support and belief in this project.

Sarah Jubar, former editor at Rowman & Littlefield, reached out to us after attending one of our presentations at the National Council for Teachers of English Annual Convention. She expressed interest in the work and encouraged us to develop and submit a prospectus for this book, which at the time we had not yet fully conceptualized. We are so appreciative of Sarah's vision and patience in working with us throughout the early stages of developing this book. Related, we are grateful for the understanding and support of the editorial team at Rowman & Littlefield, especially Tom Koerner and Carlie Wall. Thank you for helping us share the stories and experiences of rural English teachers with a broader audience.

We also want to give a shout out to our colleagues—Cathie English, Susan Martens, Robert Mitchell, Patrick Hampton, Alex Panos, Jennifer VanDerHeide, Deb Bieler, Nadia Behizadeh, and Noah Golden—for their critical feedback on early drafts of several chapters from this book. They helped us sharpen our attention to our audience—namely future and practicing English teachers—and they pushed us to continuously return to questions of relevancy and voice. We also thank Aaron Padgett for his assistance in later stages of this book. We also want to thank Valerie Kinloch for offering her perspective to open this book. The two of us had been wanting to collaborate with Valerie for quite some time, so we are so grateful for her wisdom being part of this project.

Rob wants to thank his first English Education colleague at Montana State, Dr. Lisa Eckert. She, more than anyone, helped him start to see and understand the need for paying attention to rurality as an issue of social justice. Related, Rob is grateful for the National Council for Teachers of English Standing Committee on Research (chaired by Dr. Django Paris at the time) for inviting him to present on Critical Rural English Pedagogy at the annual convention in 2015. This opportunity facilitated an understanding of the need for this work in a way and at a scale he had not fully understood previously.

On a more personal level, Rob thanks his academic colleagues over the years (too many to name!) and mentors for inspiration and reminding him why he got into this business in the first place; his close personal friends (especially Matt Helm, Roberto Amado Cattaneo, Bob Gibney, Brian Pope, Paul Goldsmith, Kevin Asselin) for being such amazing support; his crazy and very metro-centric family for always keeping things interesting; and, of course, his chosen family, Melissa Horner and Koy Marie, who make everything worth it. So much love and gratitude for y'all!

During Allison's college graduation weekend, her mom showed her a newspaper ad for a rural teaching job in Minnesota and said, "I think you should apply." What began as a seemingly random job in an unknown location turned out to be a brilliant suggestion, as Allison now holds a deep respect for teaching the English Language Arts in rural schools. Though living and teaching for nine years on the Minnesota plains made clear that the prairie was not *her* place, Allison absolutely found her people: Toni Beebout-Bladholm, Denise Kaupang, Marcy Nuytten, Brenda Palsma, Jean Duffy, Karen Hartke, Stephanie Lundberg, Josie Laleman, Judie Fox, Sandi Swartz, and Deb Ahmann. Collectively, these witty, strong, intelligent women welcomed Allison into thriving, supportive communities, and helped her navigate the landscape of teaching English in rural communities. All of her students helped shape her as well and yet, Laker Nation will forever have her heart; she is grateful for all the connections that continue. Being able to amplify the voices of students and teachers living rural now *almost* makes her commutes to and from school in the winter worth it!

Allison also thanks her colleagues who mentor her as she continues to learn the theoretical terrain of rural education and appreciates those who seek her out for collaborations. She is proud to be a rural English educator. Through it all, Allison is amazed at how her family continues to juggle life's demands and detours. Kris, Sora, and Kavi: You three are my favorites. Thank you for your encouragement, your humor, and your hugs. My courage stems from your support, and I am grateful to forever learn and explore with you.

Together, we (Rob and Allison) are indebted to the many English Education students who moved through the teacher education program we spearheaded at Montana State. These students, particularly those who went on to begin their careers in rural and remote schools, are the driving force behind this project and book. We see you, we value you, and we support what you do in rural communities and with rural students.

Finally, we are beyond grateful to and for the many rural English teachers we interviewed and spent time with during our time researching rural English Education. We found ourselves overwhelmed at times during our research by the warmth, graciousness, intelligence, resiliency, and depth of the rural English teachers we interviewed. The welcome we received was unprecedented, and we keep sacred the space you all helped create in sharing your stories with us. Spending time with these teachers changed us for the better well beyond our academic pursuits—and for this, we are truly indebted. We hope this book does justice to these teachers, their students, and the rural communities where they live.

Part I

WHY A CRITICAL RURAL ENGLISH PEDAGOGY?

Chapter 1

Moving Toward a Critical Rural English Pedagogy

Robert Petrone and Allison Wynhoff Olsen

Teaching English in Rural Communities is a much-needed book in English Education given the field's scant attention to rural contexts, classrooms, and curricula (Eckert & Alsup, 2015). Moreover, the attention that has been given to rurality within the field mainly focuses on the research community and rarely has secondary English teachers as its intended audience. In other words, for English teachers in rural and remote contexts, little exists within the professional literature for them to read about the intersection of rurality and English curriculum and instruction.

Given this situation, our hope is that this book will function as a space whereby rural English teachers can "see themselves" and their experiences reflected back to them in scholarship written not only about them but also for them. In addition, by including practicing English teachers in the writing of this book (several chapters are coauthored with rural English teachers), this book offers a "from the ground up" and accessible approach to insert, humanize, and recalibrate the place of rural teachers and contexts within English Education.

Thus, this book is meant to redress a lack of attention to rurality and join a mounting body of scholarship that recognizes the unique challenges English teachers face in rural and remote contexts (e.g., Azano, 2011, 2014; Azano & Stewart, 2015; Brooke et al., 2003; Comber, 2016; Eckert & Alsup, 2015; Eckert & Petrone, 2013).

Teaching English in Rural Communities has the potential to become an especially important resource for rural English teachers given how rampant professional isolation is for many of these teachers. The isolation of rural and remote English teachers stems both from geography and, what we refer to as, the "silo" effect of small and/or single-person English departments in many rural schools. As a result, the reality is that rural English teachers often lack disciplinary colleagues and consequently, content-specific pedagogical conversations (Wynhoff Olsen & Branch, 2018).

This book, by emphasizing concrete examples of classroom practice, provides some of this collegial dialogue in the form of ideas for rural English curricula practiced by rural English teachers in rural schools. In fact, the primary purpose of *Teaching English in Rural Communities* is to help English teachers develop equity-oriented pedagogical practices that both address broad cultural discourses of rurality and respond to the local rural contexts in which they teach.

It is important to note, too, that reading about and understanding rural contexts is essential for *anyone* invested in English Education. As an English Education colleague who focuses on urban education recently said to us, "I—and people who do what I do—need to know about this, too!" We agree. Understanding rurality is not just for people who work and live in rural contexts, particularly as urban-rural divides both potentially polarize (as evidenced by the 2016 presidential election) and promise to unite (as evidenced by many movements linking urban and rural people together to work toward common aims).

Emphasizing rurality for people beyond rural communities is crucial, too, since deficit-laden stereotypes and representations of rural people and places dominate popular culture and media. (See the next section for more on this issue.) Given these troubling depictions, it becomes imperative that teachers provide a way for students who both do *and* do not live, experience, or understand rural to have tools to speak back to these diminished representations. In this way, we see the attention to and nuanced understandings of rural contexts for teaching and learning English as crucial threads to be stitched into the broader tapestry of helping bring about a more equitable educational system for *all* students across rural, suburban, and urban contexts.

Furthermore, alongside the limited scholarship focused on rurality in English Education, attention to rural contexts for learning and teaching English is vital given the social justice concerns and issues of equity inherent in rural education (Eckert & Petrone, 2013). These social justice concerns include, among other issues, inadequate resources, poverty, shifting demographics, geographic isolation, school closures, lack of teacher support, and poor teacher retention (Azano, 2015; Bittle & Azano, 2016; Boylan & McSwan, 1998; Burton et al., 2013; Cuervo, 2016; Eckert & Alsup, 2015; McLure & Reeves, 2004; Tieken, 2014).

An emphasis on rurality is of particular importance in this current moment given the fast rate at which demographics of rural communities are changing—something that, if not attended to, often has adverse effects for students, especially those for whom English is not a first language. Moreover, though Black, Indigenous, and People of Color (BIPOC) comprise approximately 20 percent of rural populations, rurality typically gets coded as "white[1]," which raises concerns about potential social erasure of rural BIPOC communities (Tieken, 2014; Valentin, 2018), not the least of which includes Indigenous[2] populations, especially those residing on reservations. (See chapter 5 for an in-depth exploration related to the intersections of rurality and race/ism.)

TROUBLING REPRESENTATIONS OF RURALITY

Perhaps the most important purpose for writing this book, though, is to help work against the diminished representations and ideas of rurality that dominate public, and even sometimes educational, discourses. A recent line of scholarship in education has demonstrated how mainstream understandings of rurality are typically deficit oriented (e.g., Azano, 2015; Brooke, 2003; Donehower et al., 2007; Eppley, 2010; Heldke, 2006; Schafft & Jackson, 2010). Specifically, this scholarship shows that rural people and places are often thought of as lacking in many ways, not the least of which is education. Moreover, this research shows that anti-rural prejudice deems rural people as ignorant, backward, and sheltered with their ways of knowing as undesirable and unnecessary in modern society.

In these ways, rural people and ways of life are systematically marginalized and devalued to the extent that this marginality typically "goes unremarked, even unbelieved" (Heldke, 2006, p. 158). For instance, phrases such as "redneck" often get inserted into public discourse without any critique or question; in fact, the term tends to be used comically and/or matter of factly. This degradation of rural allows "pejoratives and negative stereotypes to persist in our social consciousness despite a climate of political correctness" (Azano, 2015, p. 268).

In light of the harmful stereotypes associated with rurality, it is worth considering: Who is being allowed to tell the story of rurality? Who has the power to shape the ways that rural people are perceived?

Given their marginalized status, the power for creating ideas of their place does not lie solely in the hands of rural people; thus, dominant discourses of rurality have potential to become a dangerous "single story" (Adichie, 2009) written (mostly) by non-rural people. As Schafft and Jackson (2010) argue, "All rural dwellers are nevertheless recipients of the messages from the dominant culture regarding what it means to be rural" (p. 18). Hence, reductive identities can result—both for rural people and for non-rural people to "know" rurality—and stereotypes developed and reified.

As with other marginalized categories of representation, one major concern is that these prevalent negative stereotypes can facilitate a type of "stereotype threat" (Steele & Aronson, 1995) whereby people actualize the stereotypes of the social groups to which they belong. Stereotype threat becomes tangible for rural dwellers as they are bombarded with narratives of their so-called backwardness, stupidity, and irrelevance. Steele and Aronson argue, "When the stereotype demeans something as important as intellectual ability, this threat can be disruptive enough, we hypothesize, to impair intellectual performance" (p. 808). Hence, a self-fulfilling prophecy of sorts can easily become established for rural peoples. (See Sarigianides et al., 2017 for how dominant ideas of adolescence similarly function in the lives of youth.)

For many rural people, stereotype threat has already been realized: "Somewhere along the way, rural students and adults alike seem to have learned that to be rural is to be sub-par, that the condition of living in a rural locale creates deficiencies of various kinds—an educational deficiency in particular" (Schafft & Jackson, 2010, p. 17). It is not surprising, therefore, that a prominent discourse among many rural people focuses on getting out, "escaping," and leaving rural places—typically for the promise of education and economic opportunities to be found in urban centers. This helps to facilitate the out-migration of youth from rural communities and the consequent "brain drain" that is currently challenging many rural contexts in the United States (Carr & Kefalas, 2009).

The notion of rural as being less than or irrelevant in modern life is established not only in the ways rural people see—or fail to see—themselves in media and public discourse but also in curricula used in their classrooms (Azano, 2014; Eppley, 2010). In this way, schools, too, often contribute to diminished renderings of rural.

At the secondary level, for example, while some canonical novels are set in rural contexts, albeit past/historic settings, and focus on rural characters (e.g., *Of Mice and Men, To Kill a Mockingbird*), rarely is rural itself a point of focus—and if so, even more rarely in any flattering way. In fact, continuously offering portrayals of rural as primarily historic has the potential to further facilitate a rendering of rural as something from the past and not pertinent in the present and future. Overall, this curricular tradition of disregarding or diminishing rurality is reflective of a "pedagogy of erasure" which Eppley (2011) identifies as "the unintentional practice of erasing cultural identity through neglect by not noticing and engaging the cultural practices of the other" (p. 3).

WHAT IS A CRITICAL RURAL ENGLISH PEDAGOGY?

In response to the marginalization, misrepresentation, and misunderstanding of rurality within mainstream American consciousness, politics, and, sometimes, education, we proffer a *Critical Rural English Pedagogy* framework for developing and implementing English curricula that centers rurality as an analytic focus for critical literacy practices. More specifically, a Critical Rural English Pedagogy (CREP) is meant to: (a) facilitate students' analyses and critique of discourses and ideologies related to rurality within language, texts, and society; and (b) foster students' abilities to create and dissemintate texts that re-present more comprehensive, accurate, and socially just renderings and notions of rurality, and rural people and places.

In these ways, a CREP, like other critical literacy approaches (e.g., Morrell et al., 2013) emphasizes textual consumption, production, and distribution in order to draw attention to power dynamics, representation, ideologies, social justice/equity issues, and activism. Drawing upon the foundational scholarship of Brazilian educator, Paulo Freire, whose earliest work emphasized rural communities and peoples (Freire, 1970), a CREP offers a way to facilitate students' reading and writing "the word and world" with particular emphasis on rurality.

The key underlying premise of a Critical Rural English Pedagogy to Critical Rural English Pedagogy is that the very idea of rural is a *social construct*. Similar to how notions of gender, age, and race are historically contingent and socially produced, so, too, are ideas of rurality. From this organizing premise, a CREP examines how notions of rurality are constructed with particular emphasis given to how language and texts factor into these socially produced notions of rurality.

Questions such as the following, for example, become central to and for a CREP: How do ideas of rural get produced? How do these ideas get reified (through language and texts)? How do these ideas get challenged and subverted? What effects do various notions of rurality have on/for the people identified as "rural"? For people not considered "rural"? Who establishes these ways of knowing rurality? Who benefits from them? And how does rural intersect with the teaching of English Language Arts?

By addressing these and related questions, a Critical Rural English Pedagogy extends many place conscious pedagogies (e.g., Comber, 2016; Gruenewald, 2003) by linking local community to broader notions and discourses of rurality. Whereas most place approaches emphasize making strategic connections between the local community and curricula or even facilitating students' critical literacy related to their local place, a CREP extends these local connections to asking what might it mean to critique the very idea of rurality itself in English classrooms. Thus, a CREP both addresses the local rural context *and* broader discursive constructions of rurality.

In these ways, a CREP calls into question the ideology of curriculum (Apple, 2004) and encourages teachers and students together to grapple with questions of power—both in their curriculum and in the broader sociopolitical world. Explicitly engaging representations and discourses of rurality within curriculum has the potential to expose and disrupt dominant ideas and to empower students to critically decode the images given to them about rurality by our society (and schools).

Moreover, a Critical Rural English Pedagogy has the potential to help students create new texts and counternarratives to affect these broader sociopolitical discourses. In doing so, teachers and students alike can begin to tell a new tale of what it means to be rural and help to stop, and perhaps even reverse, the "slow violence" (Nixon, 2011) currently being hoisted upon rural people and places, as well as the consciousness of non-rural people.

OVERVIEW OF *TEACHING ENGLISH IN RURAL COMMUNITIES*

Teaching English in Rural Communities is structured into three broad sections and six chapters. Part I of the book, "Why a Critical Rural English Pedagogy?," includes the preface and this introductory chapter, which provide the overarching rationale for the book and frame several key issues regarding rural English Education today, paying particular attention to social justice and equity issues inherent in rural contexts for teaching and learning the English Language Arts. Of prime significance in this chapter is the introduction to the framework the rest of this book will help further develop—a Critical Rural English Pedagogy.

Part II, "Inside Rural English Classrooms," includes chapters 2 through 4 and comprises the "heart" of this book. Specifically, these three chapters provide concrete, "real life" secondary English curricula that take up issues pertinent to a CREP. Importantly, these chapters are co-written with practicing teachers and center their classroom experiences and their personal stories. As such, they offer readers entry into each teacher's unique context and the ways in which they bring to life their iteration of a CREP that attempts to engage their students in interrogating local issues and broader social constructions of rurality.

In chapter 2, "We Ain't Much to Look At: Teaching about Rurality through Literary Texts," Alli Behrens, a teacher in the mountains of Montana, opens the door to her classroom to share a unit of study whereby she worked with students to explore how ideas of rurality are developed and shaped by media and literary texts. Specifically, she developed and then worked with her students to utilize a "Critical Rural Perspective" (Behrens, 2017), which is a concrete way to analyze texts for their representations of rural people and places.

Opening with her own experiences growing up in a rural town and feeling a diminished sense of place, Alli's curriculum is explicitly designed to equip her students with tools to make sense of the often-negative ways the media positions them as rural people. In this way, Alli's chapter emphasizes the textual consumption and power of critical analysis aspects of a CREP. Throughout this lively chapter, Alli offers practical ways to engage students in this important work, many of which can easily be adapted for different contexts.

Chapter 3, "*Who* has a 'Place' in Place-Based Pedagogy?: Indigenizing Rural English Education," takes a slightly different approach to implementing a Critical Rural English Pedagogy. Specifically, Melissa Horner explains a curriculum she developed and taught in an all-white rural context that overtly critiqued settler colonial notions of rurality as white places and spaces. To do this, Melissa centered Native American authors, texts, and issues in a curriculum that focused on issues of land, tribal sovereignty, and anti-colonialism within the context of the construction of the Dakota Access Pipeline and the Indigenous-led resistance movement to it, which is often referred to as #NODAPL.

Drawing upon her own background as not only someone who grew up in a rural community but also as a biracial (Métis/Anishinaabe and white) person, Melissa offers concrete approaches on how to Indigenize rural English Education as well as strategies on how to navigate potential student resistance to this approach. Her curriculum emphasizes critical analysis through textual consumption and includes ways to engage students in textual production as an aspect of CREP.

Chapter 4, "Linking Local Communities to Critical Rural English Pedagogies," provides a glimpse into the classrooms of two more rural English teachers—Liz Reierson and Catherine Dorian—and then offers a set of additional entry points for teachers to conceptualize developing and implementing a CREP in their unique contexts.

In her section, Liz takes the reader along the main street of the rural community where she teaches as she engages her students in a process of both celebrating and critiquing their small town. Specifically, she explains a unit that coheres around poetry; students draw upon their local community for inspiration and write and share poems to help bring about changes that might mitigate inequities and a more sustainable future for their hometown.

In this way, Liz's curriculum illuminates how a CREP does not have to attempt to encourage students to stay or leave their hometowns but rather be with the dissonance that can emerge by examining both the pride and the prejudices of one's rural community. In addition, Liz demonstrates how writing—particularly poetry—can be one way to work through this tension, as well as a way to stimulate creativity and imagine new possibilities for revitalizing rural areas.

In other words, whereas many might see reading and writing poetry as the last thing rural communities need, Liz sees it as exactly the type of work that will stoke creative and imaginative possibilities for revitalization. In doing so, Liz's curriculum shows one possibility for how a CREP can move from the textual analysis aspect of critical literacy to textual production and even distribution.

In Catherine's section, the reader is brought into a curriculum that, largely inspired by the curiosities of her students, explores the ways small rural communities can shape people's reputations in limiting ways, particularly around sexuality (e.g., slut shaming). Specifically, Catherine explains a unit of study in which students read and analyzed the controversial novel *Perma Red* as a way to engage issues of teen sexuality, reputation, and race/ism. The protagonist of the novel, Louise, is a young Native American woman growing up on a reservation who is confronted with myriad forms of oppression, including being labeled and mistreated for her perceived promiscuity.

Catherine's approach to the novel pushes the students to make sense of Louise's experiences by situating the rural context of the novel within race/ism, gender, sexuality, and settler colonialism (past and present). In this way, Catherine's curriculum illuminates how a CREP provides an opportunity for students to grapple with and see connections between various issues pertinent to both their day-to-day lives and their broader sociopolitical milieu.

Chapter 4 also offers additional ideas for teachers to move toward a Critical Rural English Pedagogy. For example, drawing upon Catherine's and Melissa's curricula, the chapter offers ways teachers might interrogate the literal land their schools sit on to learn about who the original inhabitants were to disrupt settler colonial notions of land ownership. This portion of the chapter also explores possibilities for building curricula that emphasizes a range of topics that rural English teachers have identified as especially difficult to address in their classrooms, including LGBTQIA+ issues, poverty, higher education, and alcohol and drug abuse/addition.

Building upon these three chapters, which focus on classroom curricula and instructional practices, the third section of the book, "Moving Forward," zooms out of particular classroom practices and looks at broader issues and concerns pertinent to a Critical Rural English Pedagogy.

First, chapter 5, "Re-thinking Race/ism and Rurality in English Education" explores an extremely important yet often-overlooked aspect of rurality, particularly within educational research: race. Specifically, this chapter discusses how rurality often gets coded as white, which tends to render invisible BIPOC communities in rural contexts. Additionally, this chapter explores histories and current demographic and sociological understandings of Native American, African American, and Latinx people in rural communities.

Overall, this provocative chapter pushes mainstream educational research and teachers to reconsider how race factors into their understandings of rural America. Though this chapter does not explicitly focus on curriculum, the aim is that it will inspire new pedagogical possibilities within rural English classrooms and perhaps even engender a next generation of CREP scholarship.

The final chapter of the book, chapter 6, "Opportunities and Challenges in Moving toward a Critical Rural English Pedagogy," both looks across the previous chapters as well as broadens the scope of a Critical Rural English Pedagogy beyond the classroom. Specifically, this chapter offers several strategies rural English teachers might employ when integrating their critical curricula. This chapter concludes with a discussion of how rural English teachers might look beyond their classrooms to support their participation in CREP through their engagement in practices of self-care, professional development, and sociopolitical activism.

In bringing together these chapters, *Teaching English in Rural Contexts* helps to advance the field of English Education in its aims of providing a socially just education for all students. Specifically, this book offers a conceptual framework (i.e., CREP), concrete curricular possibilities, and several ways to think beyond the classroom to promote equity in education and U.S. society writ large, particularly related to the often-deficit views of rurality that circulate in media, politics, and education.

Before moving onto the rest of this book, we pause here to draw attention to the image on the cover of the book, which was taken by Nicholas Rink, an English teacher at an alternative high school on the Blackfeet Reservation in Montana. The photo captures a group of his students during a field trip whereby they ascended Scenic Point, a peak in the Năatoōkyoōkăasii (Two Medicine) valley in what is colonially known as Glacier National Park. While scaling the peak, the students learned about geological formations and other natural phenomena in the area. The learning experience was enriched with cultural lessons and was designed to mirror cultural learning practices, placing the knowledge acquisition on mountain tops where Siksikḱaitsiittŭpiiks (*Blackfeet*) have been acquiring knowledge in ceremony since time immemorial. We selected this photo for the cover of this book because it captures what expansive possibilities of a Critical Rural English Pedagogy can look like. (This photo is used with permission from Nicholas).

NOTE

1. As a way to linguistically counter white supremacy, throughout the book, we do not capitalize the word white when used as a racial descriptor but do capitalize Black, Latino/a/x, Indigenous and Native. For more on this, we suggest the following article: Johnson, L. L. (2018). Where do we go from here? Toward a Critical Race English Education. *Research in the Teaching of English 53*(2), 102–24.

2. Throughout this book, we use the terms "Native (Peoples)" and "Indigenous Peoples" interchangeably and tribal affiliations are used when speaking about specific

examples of individuals and Nations. The P in "Peoples" is pluralized and capitalized to indicate the uniqueness of nations, groups, and cultures that have been practicing self-determination long before colonization—their inherent sovereignties do not rely on the approval of modern nation-states to recognize them as such. The terms "(American) Indian" and "Native American" are used to align with the language of laws and policies (e.g., Indian Education for All), when a cited author uses those terms, and/or when an author/contributor of this book chooses to use those terms. This nomenclature is most represented in Chapters 3, 4, and 5.

Part II

INSIDE RURAL ENGLISH CLASSROOMS

Chapter 2

We Ain't Much to Look At

Teaching about Rurality through Literary Texts

Alli Behrens, Robert Petrone, and
Allison Wynhoff Olsen

I am from an island of dirt roads and stop signs
In a sea of Ponderosa Pine.
"Blink and you'll miss it."
From limestone canyons dotted with pine trees and pictographs,
Mountain lakes and hot summer days heavy with the smell of smoke,
A cloudless blue sky, faded and blistered in the heat.

I am from the Greatest Generation,
Farmers, soldiers, singers, and Depression survivors.
Basements filled with books, baskets, and boxes,
Huckleberry-stained fingers clutching tickets to the fair.
Beaches white, glistening in the Florida sun and sand in my hair.
Popop's pancakes sizzling on the griddle
And fresh orange juice by the gallon.

I am from Peace Corp workers meeting underneath the blazing Honduran sun,
The Atlantic and Pacific joined.
Dusty cowboy boots and the musky scent of Stetson cologne,
Forest Service uniforms, a woman in leadership,
And a love that is everlasting.

I am from the soft strumming of the guitar,
"The Long Black Veil" and "How Great Thou Art"
The roar of a packed gym, sweat rolling down my face,

> "Two down, one to go!" with spring snow biting my face
> As I pull on my catcher's mitt,
> Fireworks exploding and nights of mischief and laughter,
> Running wild because fences don't matter.
>
> I am from towering pines, jagged mountains, and the bitter scent of juniper.
> From saguaros stretching their arms to the heavens
> The sky brilliant, painted with fire,
> Sunflowers nodding to me as I pass by.
> A heavy pack on my back and dusty boots on my feet.
> No matter where I wander,
> I will never forget
> Where I am from.
>
> —Alli Behrens

Heber is a small logging town in the northeastern part of Arizona, an island of houses and dirt roads in a sea of Ponderosa Pine trees. Not many people, even those who live in Arizona, have ever heard of Heber. For many years, a typical conversation prompted by "Where are you from?" (e.g., at college) would go something like this for Alli:

"I'm from Heber."
"Huh? Never heard of it. What's it by?"
"In between Show-Low and Payson."
"Hmm. I must have driven through it once or twice, just never noticed it."

After countless such conversations, Alli eventually changed her response, no longer taking time to name her hometown. Instead, she would quickly roll off her tongue, "Oh, you wouldn't know where it is. It's just a small town in the middle of nowhere." Sometimes she'd even throw in, "It doesn't matter."

For seven years, Alli taught secondary English in small rural communities in Arizona and Montana, and during that time, she worked with many students who understood her response of "Oh, it doesn't matter" when it came to locating their hometown for others. As a teacher in rural communities, these encounters pushed her to consider not only the shift she made in answering "Where are you from?" but more importantly, the underlying messages and belief systems she drew upon being from a small rural community.

Alli began to wonder: *Why did I get away from naming my hometown? Why did I buy into the notion that unfamiliarity equaled insignificance, that rural was inferior?*

As Alli began teaching, she noticed many students embodied the same negative conceptions of their hometowns and themselves because they were "rural." She noticed, also, that they wanted to be accepted for who they are, especially being from a rural context; thus, Alli felt compelled to explicitly address the idea of rurality in her classroom.

After some time, Alli began exploring various theories and scholarship of others who were similarly concerned about conceptions of rurality, particularly within English/Literacy Education (e.g., Azano, 2014, 2015; Eppley, 2010, 2011). Drawing upon this scholarship, Alli started to develop English curricula that foregrounded rurality, akin to curricula she had read about that foregrounded issues of race, class, age, gender, and urbanity (e.g., Appleman, 2009; Morrell et al., 2013). In so doing, Alli was inductively moving her teaching toward a Critical Rural English Pedagogy.

For the remainder of this chapter, Alli shares her own theoretical underpinnings—the Critical Rural Perspective (CRP) (Behrens, 2017)—and one of the curricular units she developed to implement lessons and activities focused on rurality, including how her students responded to the unit and ways teachers might adapt the CRP for their own teaching contexts. Developing and implementing this curriculum has helped her be more attuned to the value of physical place in the lives of students, their own attitudes toward it, and the ways in which the stereotypes and dominant narratives of deficit too often surround notions of rurality—including, sadly, sometimes even in the imaginations of those who identify as rural.

TEACHING CONTEXT

The curriculum discussed in this chapter took place in Whitehall, a town in Southwestern Montana. Whitehall sits near the banks of the lazy, meandering Jefferson River in wide-open, sprawling Jefferson Valley, cradled in between the Tobacco Root and Highland Mountains. Any of the iconic images from most popular Hollywood films set in Montana—from *Legends of the Fall* to *A River Runs through It* to *The Horse Whisperer*—could have easily been filmed in or near Whitehall.

Additionally, like virtually all such towns in Montana (as well as the rest of the United States), Whitehall is situated on land that was once the dominion of Native American Tribal Nations. In this case, what is currently known as "Whitehall" is embedded in what were the traditional homelands of the modern-day Confederated Salish Kootenai Tribes. Through a history of U.S. governmental sanctioned genocidal and racist policies and practices, Whitehall's current population does not include Native people and is almost entirely white.

Community

The Whitehall community consists of approximately 1,300 people "in town" with another 1,300 or so people scattered throughout the valley, or "out in the country" as it is referred to by students at the school. Given its small population, the community is tight-knit, with family trees often bending and swaying together. Hunting, fishing, four-wheeling, and archery are popular activities for Whitehall residents. Whitehall is agrarian, compiled of ranchers, miners, and forest service workers.

The town once boasted a prosperous gold mine, known as The Golden Sunlight Mine, which functioned as a main contributor to the economy due to a large number of local employees. Massive cuts in staffing levels in recent years, though, have left Whitehall hurting for industry, income, and increasingly, residents. Similar to many rural communities in Montana and other states, the future for Whitehall is uncertain and youth are often encouraged to leave or "escape" so they don't end up "stuck." (For a great exploration of this topic through the lens of high school girls' basketball, check out the documentary, *Class C*.)

School Demographics

The state database (Montana Office of Public Instruction: Growth, n.d.), at the time this chapter was written, reported 270 elementary students (K-8)—86 of whom were middle school students (6-8)—and 136 high school students (9-12), for a total of 406 students across the district. Of these students, the database indicated 93 percent of the elementary (K-8) and 90 percent of the high school students identified as white; the database did not offer racial identifiers for other students in the district, which is, of course, problematic (as will be explored in more detail in chapter 5).

Economically, the database reported 63 percent of elementary students and 40 percent of high school students as financially disadvantaged, 0 percent of students limited English proficient, and 10–14 percent of students participating in special education. Anecdotally, the majority of the students' parents are working-class ranchers, farmers, builders and mechanics. Typically, around half of graduating seniors pursue post-secondary education, but not all earn four-year college degrees. Literacy, though appreciated, is not highly prioritized in the community, as more vocational skills related to ranching, farming, and hunting often take precedence.

Like many rural areas, the secondary school is the center and "heart" of the community—the purple and gold Trojan pride appears in storefronts and on houses throughout town. The sports programs are widely supported, particularly the boys' football and basketball teams. Football games draw hundreds of excited fans, and basketball games in the gym become a gathering place for much of the community during the long, cold Montana winters.

The teaching faculty is comprised of thirteen women and five men, and of these eighteen teachers, 94 percent identify as white. Eleven of the teachers live in Whitehall and the rest commute, with a few commuting from towns as far as eighty-five miles away. Three of the teachers grew up in the Whitehall area.

In terms of their teaching assignments, it is typical for teachers to teach across middle school and high school grades, with select teachers (e.g., art/music/physical education) assigned across K-12. Alli's teaching load of six preparation periods is a prime example of teaching across grade levels and having students over time. She teaches the following: Literacy Foundations/Preparatory Middle School English; sixth grade English; seventh grade English; eighth grade English; tenth to twelfth Public Speaking; and tenth grade English. Alli has about twenty students per class.

Focal Classroom

Alli's physical classroom space is small with student desks jam-packed in the room. The walls are covered in student art, including place-based "I am From" poems (Alli's "I am From" poem begins this chapter), student identity posters, artwork, and various forms of written expression. Collectively, these artifacts indicate how Alli celebrates her students.

The "Rockstar Wall" is the decor that catches most people's eyes when they first enter the classroom. The "Rockstar Wall" has a zone for each class, on which Alli writes students' names along with an explanation of why they've become rockstars. For instance, students become rockstars for doing well on assignments, making big improvements, or for doing something great. When a class gets a certain number of rockstars, they earn a party.

While the parties are fun and offer a unique break to the school day, the greater significance of the "Rockstar Wall" is that is brokers conversations by students and teachers alike, all of whom comment on the students' accomplishments when they enter the room. As such, conversations in Alli's classroom are rich with celebrations and student voices.

Academic Aims

Alli's main curricular emphasis across grade levels is to meet students where they are, academically, with the aim of forward progress over time. Over the years, she noticed the middle school students coming from elementary school with a preference for oral storytelling and a lack of exposure to writing tasks.

Therefore, Alli emphasizes building writing stamina and adding analytical writing to students' repertoire as they move through the secondary grade levels.

Alli also prioritizes students sharing stories: stories of who they are, how they connect and clash with one another, and how they experience text-self connections. In this way, human connections, stories, and relationships are major priorities. Alli also builds classroom community with each group of students during the academic year and over time, as she teaches students for multiple years.

THEORETICAL FRAMEWORK: THE CRITICAL RURAL PERSPECTIVE

The curricular unit highlighted in this chapter was developed to draw attention to and help redress the ways conceptions of rurality and rural people, as discussed in Chapter 1, get produced and circulated—in texts and in broader sociopolitical discourses. The exigency for this unit, then, emerges from concerns that rurality suffers—like other social categories, such as adolescence (e.g., Petrone et al., 2015)—from dominant, deficit-oriented discourses with detrimental effects.

The curriculum in this chapter brings together a Youth Lens (Petrone et al., 2015) and a Critical Literature Pedagogy (Borsheim-Black et al., 2014), which asks teachers and students to center issues of ideology in teaching literary texts, foregrounding, for instance, questions such as, "Whose stories are most often told and whose are not?" (127). Specifically, the unit focuses on examining young adult literary texts that center rural characters and contexts through what is known as a "Critical Rural Perspective" (CRP) (Behrens, 2017): an analytical approach to examining ideologies within texts as they relate to rurality.

The overarching framework and the core of this unit were introducing students to and helping them utilize a Critical Rural Perspective (CRP) to examine, critique, and potentially revise portrayals and dominant systems of reasoning regarding rural in literary texts, media and popular culture texts, and in broader cultural discourses. Alli conceptualized and developed CRP as a way to provide secondary students with a practical tool or heuristic whereby they could examine texts for their implicit and explicit ideologies of rural.

The need for the CRP arises from the fact that, in the realm of critical theory, no lens exists that both questions elements of a novel "with considerations of power and oppression" (Appleman, 2009, p. 53) and challenges the societal ideologies crafting the nature of reality with regard to place, and more specifically, rural places. The CRP helps to fill the literary analysis gap regarding place and sets the stage for readers to recognize and problematize the textual construction of rurality. It brings literary elements concerning rurality into focus and helps students develop the meta-knowledge necessary for resisting and manipulating dominant discourses tied to rurality.

Concretely, the CRP focuses on characterization, setting, conflict, and theme, which are four literary elements frequently identified and analyzed in the English classroom. The CRP provides questions for students to explore those four categories when engaging in textual analysis, as well as questions for considering larger implications of textual elements. Readers can focus on a single category or consider some, or all, in conjunction. The most thorough understanding of rural representations comes from analyzing all categories together.

As table 2.1 illustrates, the CRP helps readers move from literal level of reading comprehension to deeper interpretative issues; for example, questions move from how are rural characters represented in terms of dress and talk to how is this text helping to define rural people categorically.

Table 2.1 Questions for a Critical Rural Perspective (CRP)

Critical Rural Perspective: Questions for Textual Analysis	
Characterization	Setting
1. How are rural characters portrayed in appearance, action, and intelligence?	1. How is the rural community represented?
2. How are rural youth portrayed?	2. What is the relationship between characters and their place (Are they there by choice? Do they want to stay there? Are they engaged with the community?
3. How are rural characters compared with urban characters?	
4. Who is telling the story of rural people?	
5. Do characters feel like they "belong" where they are?	3. How do the characters have influence over their place?
6. How are these representations defining rural people?	4. How is the rural setting compared with urban places in the novel?
	5. How does the setting restrict and/or privilege the characters?
	6. How are these representations defining rural places?
Plot	Theme
1. What conflicts are forefront in the novel?	1. What are the themes present in the novel?
2. What causes those conflicts?	
3. How are those conflicts resolved?	2. What ideologies do those themes convey about rural people and livelihoods?
4. Who is responsible for resolving conflicts?	
5. How do characters feel about conflict resolutions?	3. How do those themes uphold or challenge rural stereotypes?
6. What do these conflicts reveal about rural life?	

(Continued)

Table 2.1 Questions for a Critical Rural Perspective (CRP) (Continued)

Critical Rural Perspective:
Questions for Textual Analysis

Implications
1. To what extent does a person's identity depend on the rural place/space she occupies?
2. To what extent is a rural place defined by the people who occupy it?
3. Why does the novel perpetuate and/or resist rural stereotypes?
4. What textual and authorial voices are constructing the depictions of rurality? How does that impact the story told?

For each category in the CRP, readers identify the ways that rurality is depicted in the individual literary element and then analyze those representations. An important part of this work is to determine how rurality is being established in the novel and how it maps onto broader cultural depictions of rural. The last questions in each category, as well as the questions in the implications section, encourage readers to think about the creation of rural identity in the text.

Therefore, readers must first become consciously aware of the characterization of rural present in the novel. Then, as students consider rural depictions in the text, they search for the factors determining the portrayals of characters, places, and conflicts (e.g., narrator positionality, rural and urban comparisons, and stereotype use). In doing so, they can recognize that rural identity is a construct within the novel and does not necessarily reflect everyone's reality.

In this way, the CRP functions as an entry point for conversation and examination of rural texts and broader discourses of rurality. Of course, this set of questions is by no means exhaustive nor the only way to read for depictions of rural; however, it does provide a concrete, practical way to do this work while being grounded in the "traditional" analytical frameworks of English Language Arts.

In other words, a CRP creates a way to help students develop critical literacy specific to critiquing cultural figurations of rural at the same time it provides students opportunities to learn and deepen their understandings of core ELA concepts (e.g., literary analysis). Thus, a CRP helps students become better developed in the English Language Arts *and* more poised to affect social transformation.

The meta-knowledge gained through the CRP encourages consideration of the larger societal implications of literary rural representations. Gaining meta-knowledge about the textual creation of rural identity can make students aware of the construction of societal discourses of rurality and its typical reduction of what it means to *be* rural. Eppley (2010) establishes that textual images "structure our worlds, but also position us in our worlds . . . and that those images become a part of us, anchoring us to our identity and our place in reality" (p. 2).

Essentially, literary images can, and do, become part of sense-making—of ourselves and others. Textual identity is potent because it becomes a part of reader identity (Eppley, 2010), which situates meta-knowledge of textual identity as valuable and informative when thinking about societal identities. Thus, literary representations can also add to the establishment of dominant and nondominant discourses, as they indicate self-positions in relation to others.

For example, in many of Alli's students' reading, they discovered that urbanity is used as the standard by which rurality is evaluated. In other words, rural is portrayed as both reliant upon urban for measurement of success and lesser than urban because rural never meets the standard. Therefore, rural is positioned as less powerful in the world via these texts.

To use the CRP to confront larger societal narratives, readers first need to make themselves aware of the assembly of a novel, identifying and deconstructing the single story (Adichie, 2009), or what Deborah Appleman (2009) calls the "singular vision" (p. 21), contained in the story. That means instead of ignoring or accepting stereotypes in the text, readers identify their presence and decode them to "understand more about the ways we construct the world around us and how 'we' are constructed by others" (Eppley, 2010, p. 2). The hope is that readers can then extend their awareness of discursive identity formation in a text to the world around them, helping them "learn to read both texts and the world with a nuanced and critical eye" (Appleman, 2009, p. 10).

This consciousness can, and should, lead to resistance at both the textual and the societal levels. Students need to reject the single story of rurality which creates an image of rural that has become normal, expected, and natural; it's an image that establishes a sense of "that's just the way things are." Once students have noticed the ways identities just "are," they can question identity construction.

In doing so, students can push back against the normalized way of representing rural. Rural stereotypes are situated as reality in novels and in society, but those representations do not have to be an individual's reality. Armed with the CRP, students can defy stereotypical depictions by refusing to self-characterize in the ways dominant discourses would have them.

Students can further resist dominant discourses by questioning and challenging authorship, authority, and authenticity of representations by offering their own lived narratives. However, implementing the CRP may also make readers confront stories of rurality that they have no counternarrative for, even though they may wish they did. Both moves are vital for helping students engage with rural texts and the world in which they are situated because in order to be critical readers of place, students must engage with and examine the "uncomfortable parts" of place and identity, as "a true knowledge of place ... must address the less-than-positive characteristics" (Brooke, 2003, pp. 68–69).

It is important to note that students don't need permission to be critical of their place, and rarely do they need help to do so; and yet, by bringing their critiques into the classroom, teachers provide a platform for students' critiques, validation of their perspectives, and opportunities to discuss their ideas.

Through the use of CRP, this unit was not just about reading young adult literary texts that emphasize rurality but more so about helping students develop *a way of engaging texts through a lens to interrogate and analyze for their depictions of rurality.* Since YA novels are cultural artifacts that have the power to develop, perpetuate, and/or challenge cultural assumptions and discourses, they provide an apt platform for engaging youth in the work of examining, critiquing, and revising dominant stories of rurality. Hence, the curriculum explained in the next section offers one teacher's attempt to integrate broad perspectives on transforming our social world as it pertains to rurality into a secondary English curriculum.

THE CURRICULUM: "READING FOR RURAL" IN SECONDARY ENGLISH

As this chapter now turns to focus on the actual curriculum, it is important to acknowledge that this curricular unit was not a "one and done" experience in the classroom. As is true with multicultural texts and perspectives, integration of such key concepts must be an on-going, sustained practice within a curriculum so as to avoid the phenomenon of checking off a box for having fulfilled a requirement or a quota, something that too often equates with tokenizing groups of people or places.

Therefore, this unit, titled "Reading for Rural," was placed at the beginning of the school year and provided a broad framework for the entire course. In this way, the concepts in this unit appeared and were built upon over time.

Additionally, the unit was placed at the beginning of the school year so that the seventeen eighth graders in the English Language Arts class would know from the very beginning that their teacher knew they and their place/community were worth learning and talking about—that their stories and knowledge were valuable and worthy of study, and that their ways of being would play an integral role in the classroom and curriculum. And though the students sometimes expressed doubt that their teacher believed that their rural lives, experiences, and perspectives were connected to academia, most of them were excited by the attention, care, and focus.

Goals of the Curriculum

Given that the CRP was the core of this curriculum, much of this unit was organized to help scaffold students to learn the CRP and to practice using it in their analysis of texts. Specifically, the overarching unit goals were to help students:

- Read for (and potentially resist) implicit and explicit ideologies within/of texts related to representations of "rural";
- Consider larger societal implications of characterization, setting, plotline, and theme;
- Question authorship and "authenticity" of rural narratives;
- Provide opportunities to think and write analytically about media and literary representations, physical characteristics of place, and community culture and practices.

To reach the aims of the unit, students completed four major tasks alongside a variety of smaller activities designed to scaffold toward these major tasks:

1. Writing personal poetry of place (i.e., "Where I'm From" poem);
2. Learning the CRP and applying it to a choice YA novel that focused on rural characters and places;
3. Developing and writing a literary analysis;
4. Crafting a personal narrative that moved the CRP from textual analysis to more personally pertinent questions and issues.

Each of these sections of the unit is explained in detail in table 2.2.

Section #1: Thinking about Culture and Representation

The first section of the unit focused on opening up broad topics and issues, such as culture, representation, and stereotype. The culminating task was the writing and sharing of "Where I am From" poems. Below is an explanation of several activities and smaller assignments that helped scaffold the students to learn related concepts and generate their poems.

Identifying (Rural) Culture

The unit opened with a deliberate proclamation: "Your views and your stories matter just as much as other people's stories do." From there, the unit shifted into conversations and activities about "culture." The class defined the word culture and discussed the elements that come together to create a culture, such as food, dress, celebrations, and beliefs.

A purpose in making this move so early in the unit was the desire to get students to think about and discuss their own culture as Whitehall residents,

Table 2.2 Tasks and Activities

Major Section and Task		Supporting Activities	
1. Thinking about Culture and Representation	Culture Posters: Whitehall Montana Rural	Stereotypes: Boys versus Girls and Chimamanda Adichie "The Danger of a Single Story"	Constructing the Grand Narrative of Rural: What Does Society Say?	Round Robin Peer Responding
Writing a "Where I'm From" poem				
2. Analyzing Rural	Critical Rural Perspective (CRP)	Book Tasting and selection	Weekly Check-ins and discussion	Student-selected vocabulary words
Reading a Young Adult novel with a rural setting				
3. Producing Rural	Thesis statements and outlining	MLA citations	Written argument (Lunchroom Murder)	Round Robin Peer Responding
Writing a literary analysis				
4. Making it Personal	Plot chart and developing conflict in narrative	Word Choice and voice	Sentence Structure	Round Robin Peer Responding
Writing a personal narrative				

Montanans, and rural people. To do this, the students worked in groups of two or three to make lists on posters that articulated the culture of Whitehall, the cultures of Montana as a whole, and the cultures of rural communities writ large. Each of the three topics—Whitehall, Montana, and rural communities—had a designated color for the poster.

Once students completed their lists, they presented their ideas to the class. Students compared ideas across groups, adding elements that had been missed but discovered in whole class debriefing. A key feature of these discussions was the idea that culture is not a static entity but is ever-evolving and is defined differently by different people.

In many ways, this activity was one of the most difficult parts of the entire unit. Some of the students struggled to identify the elements of their lives that shape them and since many of them had not spent much time outside of the community, they didn't necessarily know what made them unique. They had never been asked to think or talk about it before.

In fact, to get the ball rolling, Alli had to point out some of what she noticed upon moving to Whitehall that was different from the small town in Arizona in which she had grown up. The students couldn't believe that their teacher had never had a pasty until moving to Whitehall, and in fact, she didn't even know how to pronounce the word properly until someone corrected her! As the class talked about the role of that specific food in the culture of the community, they were able to articulate other aspects of their lives that make up the culture of their place.

Before concluding the conversation about culture, Alli admitted to her students that the culture of the area was different than what she had envisioned based on things she had read in books and seen in movies about Montana. This conversation about culture and their teacher's status as an "outsider" in the community, given that she had lived there for *only* seven years, was helpful in moving the class into the next teaching activity: a discussion of stereotypes.

Stereotypes

The second major teaching activity in the unit focused on stereotypes. Since there are many stereotypical representations of rurality present, the goal was to help students think about how stereotypes might come about, how they might be hurtful, and how they might be inaccurate. In order to do this, the class first defined stereotype. Then, they discussed why stereotypes might come into existence.

Though the students had some ideas, many returned to the idea that stereotypes exist because "that's the way those people are!" Little did they know, they were walking into the perfectly laid trap of the curriculum. In fact, these comments worked well to help deepen inquiry.

To start the process of delving deeper, the class began by focusing on gender stereotypes. After discussing the problematic nature of dichotomizing gender at all, the class split into different groups along self-ascribed gender categories and each group was asked to tell what they "knew" about the other as a group. Alli listed their ideas on the board without comment, and the side being described was asked to sit quietly and listen. The listeners were, unsurprisingly, in a rage because while there were some positive stereotypes listed, most were negative.

The girls, for example, were angry when the boys said that "girls aren't strong or good at sports" and immediately challenged the boys to a basketball game. The boys were irate when the girls said that "boys aren't as good at school" or that "they are messy," with one boy pulling a quiz he had recently aced out of his immaculate three-ring binder.

Once the students settled, their emotional response created the opportunity to remind them that what is true for one or many does not equate with what is true for all and just because it's true for one person, that doesn't mean it has to be true for you. This was an activity, albeit not without problems, that began to move the concepts of the unit from ideational to personal and tangible. The class then watched Chimamanda Ngozi Adichie's (2009) TED talk, "The Danger of a Single Story" and discussed the danger of relying on stereotypes when thinking about other people and also when thinking about ourselves.

Media Representations of Rural

The third activity focused on societal ideas of rural culture through representations from movies, music, advertisements, and other media. Alli shared media samples (e.g., The Beverly Hillbillies and ads with people speaking in undecipherable, thick accents) and students reacted with comments such as the following: "Geez, that makes us look dumb." When students shared media samples, many brought in positive representations of themselves as rural people (e.g., beautiful ranch ads), revealing students' deep pride for where they are from. While Alli was pleased that her students were able to find portrayals that they felt accurately represented them, she was surprised that they did not bring in the negative portrayals of rural—given how dominating these representations are. As she considered what this might mean, she wondered about the extent to which her students were (un)aware of the ways rural is represented in demeaning ways.

This contrast between students' own representations of themselves and a dominant perception of rurality yielded important conversations. The class wondered how outsiders may understand rural when they lacked firsthand knowledge of the lifestyle and thus, their conversations stimulated thought about how powerful positive portrayals could be generative to shift cultural discourses, particularly through the students' own textual production.

Getting Personal

After discussing others' representations of rurality, the students were asked to represent, from their perspectives, where they were from. One of the goals was to create space for students to express how they truly see themselves. This took the form of a "Where I'm From" poem based on George Ella Lyon's version. This assignment was met with an unsurprising amount of groaning as students voiced, "Poetry is the worst!" and "I can't write poems." Fittingly, one of the great pedagogical values of this activity is how it helped reframe several of these perceptions toward poetry.

The assignment began with an introduction to figurative language and poetry terms. The class then read Lyon's poem and discussed what particular story that poem was telling about where Lyon was from. Next, students began brainstorming for their own poems using the five senses as categories for ideation. Students listed things such as "steak sizzling," "fresh-cut hay," and "sweaty gym socks" for scent; "giant mountains," "rusty truck," and "the giant M on the mountain" for sight.

While students were not required to focus on physical place in their poems, most focused on the beauty of where they live to flesh out their visions of where they are from, writing about ranches they live on and the old homesteads they drive by regularly. One student, Alex, wrote the following stanza for his poem:

> I am from mountains,
> From mowing and melodies from the 80's.
> I am from the towering sunflower patch,
> Like skyscrapers,
> waving hello in the wind.
> I am from the gentle gurgle of the creek,
> Whose every eddie
> and current I've explored.

Alex took this assignment seriously, meticulously searching the thesaurus for the right words to capture the image he desired. Proud of his work, Alex wanted to submit it to the Montana State Fair.

Another student, Marie, wrote the following stanza for her poem:

> I am from old tractors,
> From slow two lane traffic.
> I am from the sound of an
> old truck engine

> (Rusty, smelling
> of old diesel)
> I am from the long
> Afternoons spent in the
> Lofty, isolated mountains.

Marie was a wildly different student than Alex. She was not confident in her writing abilities; in fact, she had confided at the beginning of the year that she wasn't good at English, so she shouldn't be expected to do well. In the end, she became one of the strongest writers in the class, which, in many ways, started with this poem. When her poem was done, Marie was thrilled with what she had come up with and was beaming about it.

After students drafted, peer-responded, revised, and finalized poems, Alli hung their work in the hallway for others to read. Students and teachers alike stopped to read the poems and compliment the writers. At the end of the school year, the students remarked that writing these poems and reading their classmates' poems was one of their favorite activities from the year, and it seems that a key reason was that they were able to "publish" their work and receive validation for it from readers other than the teacher.

The poems stayed hanging on the walls the entire school year to help remind the students, as they delved into place, that so much of what was happening in the classroom that year was developed and shaped by where they are from—that their place mattered.

Section #2: Analyzing Rural

Building upon the previous section of the course, this second section delved deeply into analyzing text for representations of rural. This portion of the unit marked the "turn" from thinking about broad ideas of representation and stereotypes to examining how texts function ideologically, particularly related to rurality. A key component of this section was the introduction of the CRP. The culminating task was to read a YA novel focused on rural characters and places and apply the CRP.

Reading for Rural

The fifth, and most time-consuming, activity of the unit was the "Reading for Rural" assignment. After dabbling in reading, analyzing, and authoring rural representations in the first section of the unit, the students were ready for a bigger, more sustained project. For this assignment, each student was required to select and read a novel that focused on a rural setting and characters. The only other requirement was that each student read a different book.

This activity began with Alli bringing in a cart full of 40, preselected novels, all of which were young adult novels with rural settings (see table 2.3 for a sampling of titles). Many of these novels had contemporary settings, which can be challenging to find. In fact, many of the students noted that there weren't many books on the cart, with one student remarking, "It looks like people aren't really writing about rural places."

(We challenge you to pause reading and think of as many YA novels you know of that focus on contemporary rural characters; when you are finished, we encourage you to repeat this exercise with a focus on contemporary urban characters. Our sense is that you'll likely be able to conjure many more books focused on urban than rural, which illuminates the marginality of rurality, including within curricula, as discussed in chapter 1.)

All of the books in table 2.3 were approved for the eighth graders to read. While some of the novels were not school-approved for middle schoolers in general, students in this class had parent permission to read novels from the high school side of the library. It is thus important for other teachers to note that Alli chose some of the novels specifically for these particular students because their parents allowed them to have access to books that take up more complex issues; however, she found that selecting books with

Table 2.3 Sampling of Novels

Title	Author	Year Published
Bastard out of Carolina	Dorothy Allison	1992
Dead End in Norvelt	Jack Gantos	2011
Necessary Roughness	Marie G. Lee	1991
Only Love Can Break Your Heart	Ed Tarkington	2016
Hattie Big Sky	Kirby Larson	2006
Bull Rider	Suzanne Williams	2009
The Absolutely True Diary of a Part-Time Indian	Sherman Alexie	2007
The Last Buffalo Hunter	Jake Mosher	2000
The Last Exit to Normal	Michael Harmon	2008
The Miseducation of Cameron Post	Emily Danforth	2012
My Life with the Walter Boys	Ali Novak	2014
Schooled	Gordon Korman	2007
Badd	Tim Tharp	2011
Knights of Hill Country	Tim Tharp	2006
Far from Xanadu	Julie A. Peters	2005
Dairy Queen	Catherine G. Murdock	2006
The Off Season	Catherine G. Murdock	2008
Front and Center	Catherine G. Murdock	2009
Hope was Here	Joan Bauer	2000
The Queen of Kentucky	Alecia Whitaker	2012
Touch Blue	Cynthia Lord	2010
Dumplin'	Julie Murphy	2015
The Serpent King	Jeff Zentner	2017

contemporary rural settings for younger students was a challenge, as they are not as prevalent.

Once the books were in the classroom, the students scattered them on desks around the room and engaged in a "Book Tasting." Specifically, each student read (or "tasted") excerpts from a minimum of four books and then explained the one book they would like to read. Students enjoyed sampling multiple novels and appreciated that the novel they would read in full was their choice. Allowing students to choose their novels helped also reaffirm the ethos in the class that students' interests mattered. It also is significant that the student choice also promoted a joint exploration of rural; this unit was not about the teacher deciding one representation to offer the class.

After students chose their novels, there was a discussion about reading logistics. Establishing expectations was crucial, particularly since students had a significant amount of autonomy during the novel portion of the unit, and assessing their work and comprehension was going to be more challenging than if everyone was reading the same book. Also, because Alli had previous experiences with eighth graders not always exhibiting the best organizational and time-management skills, the assignment was quite structured.

Each student's reading schedule was broken down into four "chunks"— one for each of the four weeks they were given to complete their novels. In the end, Alli's anxiety to control the reading was mostly unwarranted, as students' engagement trumped the assessment parameters established for them. The students read with gusto, unlike most of the previous experiences she had with students reading at that school.

In discussions about their engagement, students explained that they were excited to read because they got to choose their book and—more significantly—because the novels they were offered were all set in rural places telling stories about rural kids. As such, they were reading stories that were versions of their own lives. They didn't have to be spectators—they could be a part of the narratives, and so they read well beyond what was required of them. In fact, they read quicker and more deeply.

Once students had novels in front of them, the CRP was introduced, which brought the focus fully into teaching students how to read analytically. Generally, students understood that they would be reading novels of their choice for characterization, setting, plot, and theme. A good deal of time was spent talking about how to use the CRP as a tool to guide their thinking and interpretation.

To do this, students were given a copy of the specific questions developed for how to read for rural using the CRP (table 2.1) and analysis was explained as the following: "All we are doing is breaking down what we see and trying to figure out what all these different pieces mean. We are trying to separate things out so we can try and come up with a conclusion." Then, the group practiced using the CRP with a passage from Catherine G. Murdock's *Dairy Queen* before moving onto their individual novels.

In retrospect, more practice on shorter pieces would help better scaffold students before they turn to their own book; in fact, it might be useful to consider starting with a single text for the entire class and then transitioning to individual choice texts.

Once the students had a grasp on the CRP, they read independently. They set their own weekly goals for reading pace and had time during class to read. Students tracked their progress and practiced reading with the CRP, jotting their ideas on the "Reading for Rural Check-in" required each week (see figure 2.1).

At the end of every week, students moved into groups of three or four and discussed what they had found in their reading, comparing and contrasting the representations of rurality found in their novels. At this point, using the CRP was more about the identification of representations than actual analysis. The analysis of what the text meant came after students finished their entire novels.

Reading and discussing the novels took four school weeks, time that was sped up due to student engagement with the novels. During this time, there were several mini-lessons on literary elements, analysis, vocabulary, and grammar. For example, students explored the characterization of a single character in their novels and Alli used that as an opportunity to teach indirect versus direct characterization, character development, character motivation, and character analysis. Even with the mini-lessons, most days students had at least twenty minutes of class time to read.

Several students read their books at a much faster pace than was expected, so those who finished their novels just grabbed a new book and continued reading and participating. One student shared, "I had never found a book I liked to read" and was in awe that he was both reading his book in full and was enjoying it.

This level of engagement born from giving a rural kid a rural novel is perhaps best exemplified by Matthew. Matthew had made sure, as this assignment was handed out to the students, to inform Alli that he did not read books and that he certainly was not planning on starting now. And yet, during the Book Tasting assignment, Matthew surprised himself by finding three different books that he wanted to read. He settled on *Bull Rider* by Suzanne Williams, and he read it in two days.

He then proceeded to read the entire *Dairy Queen* series by Catherine G. Murdock and *Queen of Kentucky* by Alecia Whitaker before the four weeks assigned for this unit concluded. After that, Matthew read through any novel

Grade for Week					
Reading: __/10	On-Task: __/10	Group work: __/10	This worksheet: __/20	Total: __/50	

Name:

Reading for Rural Check-in

Week #_____

Book Title:_____

Pages Read:_____

Pages left to read:_____

Potential Vocab words

Summary of what you have read so far:

Reading for Rural observations:

(Answer a few of the questions in each category found on the back of your RFR packet.)

Characterization	Setting

Plot	Theme

Figure 2.1 Reading for Rural Check-In Assignment Sheet. *Created by Alli Behrens.*

Alli could find that had a contemporary rural setting (until there were not any more novels for him to read). There are no doubts—between Matthew or Alli—that his pace of devouring books happened because he was given access to these rural storylines and a perspective with which to experience them.

Section #3: Producing Rural

This third section moves from a focus on reading rural to writing about rural. To make this shift, students took their notes and thoughts about their individual books and developed argument-based literary analysis papers—the major task of this section.

Literary Analysis

Once students completed their novels, Alli shifted her teaching focus to literary analysis. The purpose of the literary analysis was to answer the question: What does this novel say about culture and belonging in rural places? The students had never been asked to write anything of this nature before. Thus, Alli asking students to analyze what they had discovered as they read for rural challenged them in myriad ways.

A mystery called "The Lunchroom Murder" was used to practice analysis of evidence, thesis development, paragraph structure, and written argument. From this shared story used to focus on analytical moves, Alli then scaffolded her students to use the text of their novel as evidence; then, she asked students to draw conclusions about what their individual novels "said" about rural places.

Students used the CRP to think about their novel's representations of rural and far exceeded Alli's expectations, as well as the work previous students had done. Their work was insightful and powerful; for example, some of their thesis statements were as follows:

- "In this novel, urban places are more patterned and predictable than rural places."
- "Rural people are gritty."
- "This novel shows that just because you live in a rural community doesn't mean you can't be successful in life."
- "In the novel Dead End in Norvelt, the characterization, setting, and plot reveal that small towns are dying."
- "The characters don't feel like they belong because it's a town they want to escape."
- Small towns are places where "nobody stays unless they get pregnant or have a family business to take over."
- "When rural people go to town they forget what's truly important to them."

And, with the help of the CRP, the students had quite a lot of evidence from the text to support their conclusions.

When the CRP is put into practice, the results will not be homogenous, which surprised Alli at first. She had read the majority of the novels her students read, and she expected the students to view the representations of rurality the same way she did. As she discussed the students' ideas and interpretations with them, she understood that in many ways, while she was desperate for rural to be recognized and talked about in these stories, she was using the CRP from a "metrocentric" standpoint. She was paying attention to rurality, but she was still hindered by the metrocentric thinking that shapes the way rurality is typically portrayed.

As a result of reading her students' analyses, she realized this: the CRP brings attention to the representations of rural, but the interpretation of those representations lies with the reader and will be a result of her/his worldview. Knowledge-making lies within the students, as it should. This is their lens, and these are their voices and their stories.

Section #4: Making It Personal

The final section of the unit asked students to shift from consumers to producers of text. Specifically, Alli used students' experiences reading and analyzing representations of rural produced for them as a foundation; she then taught them how to examine their lived experiences to produce their own narratives of rural. The major task of this section of the unit is a personal narrative. This demonstrates how an important aspect of Critical Rural English Pedagogy is to help students recognize the power of language and literacy to craft their own representations and narratives of rurality.

Personal Narrative

The last assignment for this unit was a personal narrative: an opportunity for students to tell their own stories of what it means to be rural. The prompt for the assignment was the following: Write a personal narrative that tells a story of what it means to *be* in this town.

Alli's students dove into this assignment, excited for the opportunity to write something that wasn't "academic" and that was all about them. They wrote about starting middle school, moving away from Montana, making friends, being a cowboy, playing soccer, and spending time with family. Carey wrote about moving to Whitehall from a Southern city:

> Two days had passed and we showed up in Whitehall, a small town in Montana with barely anything, but a couple of small stores. I wasn't looking forward to be living here for who knows how long, but I knew I didn't have a choice. We showed up at my grandma's 5 minutes later and I bolted inside not wanting to

unpack anything. I left all my bags in the back of my mom's truck. I left it this way so it would be easier for me to leave with her in a couple days. I was not going to stay here in this boring town.

Sports are a big part of the culture of Whitehall, and Hannah wrote about her experiences with basketball:

I wanted to be with the older girls and hang out with them, but the older girls didn't need me. They didn't need me because they already had what they wanted which was each other. It's not that they didn't want me, I just felt awkward around them which didn't help at all. This is a big reason I think I always ended up with the people who weren't at my level in basketball. If I was ever with one of the older girls, it was because their partner was gone. They didn't want to be stuck with the not-so-good basketball players. I was always lonely, and other than playing the game, I wasn't happy.

Brent wrote about his experience of moving away from Montana for several years:

I didn't feel the same there because there weren't really any country kids there, like there were in Montana. I went through school acting like I belonged but inside I really didn't belong. When my friends would try to do something I just went along like I was enjoying myself, like laughing even though it wasn't funny, but I really wasn't. I liked the school program but not really the kids in the school. After one year of battling my way through school, a kid finally came that was a cowboy just like me. I was so excited for this, and of course, we very quickly became friends. From then on, I thought that I was going to be comfortable, and finally fit in there, but at that time we were experiencing different problems on the ranch.

The personal narratives the students wrote depict triumphs and challenges, joy and pain, beauty and ugliness. Students identified what they love about where they live, as well as things they are not thrilled about. Their stories were honest, funny, heartwarming, and sad. Similar to their use of the CRP, their narratives revealed that the perceptions of their shared rurality differ. What it means to *be* rural is defined by the lived experiences of the individual as they are situated within the whole of the community.

The unit culminated in the sharing of these narratives and the students' reflections on rural—from those produced *for* them to those *they* produced.

CONCLUSION

In Alli's classroom, this unit started a programmatic journey of exploring place, students' identities as rural people, and notions of rurality as a concept in general. This unit was not a single, stand-alone exploration that was completed at unit's end; rather, students' use of the CRP during this unit was an entry point into continued uses of this and other critical lenses in her classroom. Using a form of critical literacy that was close to home, Alli facilitated deep student engagement with reading and writing, and she established a classroom community ethos of relevancy and purpose.

The CRP makes the invisible visible, so to speak, which is no easy feat for students who are used to reading texts for basic comprehension tests or book reports. And yet, Alli enacted the stance that her students were capable, co-constructors of knowledge. She also made recursive moves to question and modify their uses of CRP throughout the academic year.

Alli's development and integration of a unit designed to help students critique representations of rurality in literary texts is a prime example of a Critical Rural English Pedagogy in action. Specifically, this chapter illuminates how an English curriculum can move beyond a focus on local place by extending to broader discursive renderings of the idea of rurality.

Moreover, Alli's curriculum demonstrates how a CREP helps students toggle between "reading the word and the world" as they simultaneously deepen their understanding of English Language Arts skills and practices (e.g., literary analysis) and their complex understandings of how texts mediate their experiences and understandings of rurality. As English teachers consider Alli's curriculum, we encourage them to consider how they, too, might foreground critical analyses of rurality in their curricula.

Chapter 3

Who has a "Place" in Place-Based Pedagogy?

Indigenizing Rural English Education

Melissa Horner, Robert Petrone,
and Allison Wynhoff Olsen

The Four Tipi Poles of the Apsáalooke (Crow) Nation: "I have but one tipi. It has but four poles. It is held to the ground by big rocks. My east lodge pole touches the ground at the Black Hills, my south, the ground at the headwaters of the Wind River, my west, the snow-capped Absaroke and Beartooth Ranges, the north lodge pole resting on the Bearpaw Mountains."

—Two Leggings, Apsáalooke
(Crow), 1847–1923

Growing up in rural Montana, Melissa spent weekends camping in the woods in polyester, self-assembled tents, sometimes until the snow blanketed the ground in September. Then as autumn emerged, she hunted out of large canvas wall-tents during archery season. And as spring appeared, she spent time playing games with her cousins in screened mesh tents in the vast fields nestled behind her auntie's house. Tents, and the space a tent provides to access alpine forests, animals, and the intricacies of nature, were touchstones throughout her life experiences of and in the rural place she is from—Montana.

Melissa is not the first or only member of her family to have an early relationship with tents or "rurality." Her mother relays the single-sentence story as: "Well, you know, grandma was born in a tent." Melissa's maternal grandmother was born in a "tent" because her relatives were born in "tents" longer than anyone can remember.

The part of this story Melissa did not understand until she learned more about her maternal family's Métis/Turtle Mountain Anishinaabe identities and the impacts colonization had on them was that the "tent" her grandmother was born in is also called a *mikiiwaap* or what most descendants of settler colonists know of as a *tipi*. Additionally, the "rurality" Melissa knows today—connected to her own tent experiences, vast wildernesses, and sparse density between people and manmade structures—is a different "rurality" than her Métis/Turtle Mountain Anishinaabe grandmother and Native ancestors experienced a generation and more ago.

Melissa's background, particularly the geographic and biracial components of her identity (Métis/Anishinaabe and white), contribute to the ways she chooses to teach in rural classrooms and explore understandings of rurality. Subsequently, from her own life and familial inspiration, she has come to view "rural" as embedded within larger frameworks of settler colonialism, (cultural) genocide, the creation of Native reservations, self-determination for Native Peoples, and tribal sovereignty, among other elements.

It is through this approach to rurality that Melissa designed curricula for her English Language Arts courses. Specifically, she sought to create curricula that would broaden and deepen notions of rural people and spaces in a way that would move toward a more complete representation of the actual People and lived realities across rural spaces.

Montana is in the top five states across the nation with the highest per capita numbers of Native Peoples—comprising 7 percent of the total population (U.S. Census Bureau, 2018). Being from a state that Native folks exist in—and have since time immemorial—as leaders, hunters, teachers, chefs, community members, storytellers, scientists, and artists, it was vital to interrogate and expand conceptions of who and where is considered rural.

To do this, Melissa *indigenized* her English Language Arts teaching. As she demonstrates in the curriculum highlighted in this chapter, indigenizing her curricula meant:

1. Foregrounding texts by and about Native Peoples;
2. Making visible relationships between white students' connection to place and some Native Peoples' connection to the same places; and
3. Centering the ways in which texts, policies, and Native experiences are interwoven as a mechanism to better understand place—in this instance, the state of Montana.

Regardless of whether or not Melissa named this as an explicit emphasis on rural, just by virtue of teaching Native voices and texts, she was inherently teaching about rurality. These perspectives and texts are still often marginalized or excluded altogether in classroom curricula even despite some states, legislation that mandates K-12 educators include Native texts and perspectives in curriculum.

For example, the state of Montana has as part of its state's constitution, Indian Education for All, also known as "IEFA." Despite this legislation's many successes, many students in Montana, as this chapter illustrates, do not leave high school with robust understandings of Native histories, literatures, and contemporary issues.

As she built her curriculum, given her rural and biracial identity, as well as her contemplation of how conceptions of rurality might have come to be, Melissa kept in mind inquiries of whose "place" she and her students were thinking about and discussing when they examined lands and literatures of their rural state with diverse rural people. In a broad sense, Melissa's curriculum pushes us to consider *who* has a "place" within place-focused education?

TEACHING CONTEXT

In the south-central part of Montana, the altitude and grandeur of the Rocky Mountains begin to give way to the windy vastness of the coulee-riddled plains. In the approximate six months of the year that is winter in this part of Montana, it is always possible that the Interstate-90 exit to Park City will be drifted over with snow and the town of 900 people will be completely inaccessible from the endlessly stretched Montana highway. Other entry points to Park City would be an approach from the Yellowstone River—known as the Elk River to many Apsáalooke people—to the south of town, or via one of the many dirt roads that wind through the sugar beet and corn farmlands that surround the town.

When Park City is accessible from the highway, the exit leads to the quarter-mile stretch of road that is Main Street, complete with a gas station, post office, two bars, and a library. Railroad tracks splice through Main, and these tracks are flanked on one side by stacked round-bales of hay that read "We Heart Our Panthers" in the red and black school colors that starkly contrast the golden hay. Main Street's end leads to the single building that houses Park City's elementary, middle, and high school.

Community

The Park City community turns out in droves to support students in school athletics, assemblies, and seasonal events. It is quite common, for example, that the entire town is present for the Homecoming Parade, Future Farmers of America preparations, track meets, and basketball, football, and volleyball games.

A community that is largely rooted in ranching and agriculture, it is also common that many students across classes and grade levels simultaneously miss school in order to help neighboring families, friends, and relatives during calving, branding, and harvesting seasons. Community members who do not farm and ranch often work in the neighboring towns of Laurel or Billings at the oil refinery, for the railroad, or as mechanics, among other blue-collar-type professions.

School Demographics

Like many Montana schools, Park City School District reveals the racial segregation resultant from decades-long settler colonialism that displaced Native populations across Montana and later systematically removed African American and Chinese immigrant populations through a practice known as "sundown towns" (Loewen, 2005).

Though Park City is located only 18 miles as the crow flies from the Apsáalooke (Crow) reservation, which covers 2.2 million rural acres—making it the largest reservation in Montana—Park City's community, teachers, and student bodies are predominantly White (97 percent) (Census Viewer, 2012). Additionally, Park City High School is considered a "Class C" school, a designation determined by the student population, which falls right around 150 students grades 9–12, with 18 percent grouped as economically disadvantaged, and 14 percent as special education (Montana Office of Public Instruction: Growth, n.d.).

Classroom

The high school section of the school is relegated to one hallway. Upon entering Melissa's classroom, if someone were to gaze straight ahead above the desks arranged in rows facing one another, they'd see three large posters hanging side by side. They read:

Reading the world always precedes reading the word, and reading the word implies continually reading the world. As I suggested earlier, this movement from the word to the world is always present. —Paulo Freire

There must exist a paradigm, a practical model for social change that includes an understanding of ways to transform consciousness that are linked to efforts to transform structures. —bell hooks

Our perspectives of the world are narrow and until we actively attempt to understand each other, we cannot fully appreciate or respect each other.
—Shane Bitney Crone

To the left of the posters is a board that displays "Bell Ringers," with subheadings consisting of writing, reading, grammar, and current events activities that kick-off every class period. The remainder of the classroom has numerous splashes of leafy greens woven throughout in the form of plants strategically placed to ward off the sterile feeling of generic classroom space.

Around Melissa's desk, drawings, announcements, and thank you cards from students hang interspersed with the wooden-framed photos of Melissa's international travels; her dog, Koy; and her favorite neighboring mountain range, the Crazy Mountains, known as "The Crazies" by most non-Natives, and to many Apsáalooke as the Snow-Capped or Ominous Mountains, translated as "Awaxaawippiia."

Next to Melissa's desk is the "Reading Nook," where students vie for a place during in-class reading invitations—they sprawl out on the multicolored rug, propping up with the plush cushions beneath the warm light of the reading lamp. Close to the Reading Nook is the Classroom Library, a bookcase stocked with a variety of books from Melissa's personal book collection that the students regularly sift through and borrow. Some of the most checked-out books are those that Melissa has displayed in the "What Ms. Horner is reading" list, and has included *Sundown Towns: A Hidden Dimension of American Racism* by James Loewen, *Grandmother's Grandchild: My Crow Indian Life* by Alma Hogan Snell, and *Milk and Honey* by Rupi Kaur.

In this classroom, Melissa sees about 100 of the 150 high school students over the course of the six preparation periods she's responsible for teaching each day: Speech, English 10, English 12, English 9, Journalism, and Fiction to Film. For the purposes of this chapter, one unit will be showcased from Melissa's English 10 class.

Academic Aims of Curriculum

The 8-week-long unit plan described in this chapter was situated within a broader curriculum designed under the umbrellas of critical and racial literacies. Melissa's overall aims for the tenth grade English class' year-long curriculum were twofold. The first goal was to cultivate *critical literacies* (e.g., Freire, 1970; Wallowitz, 2008)—an approach that would allow students to unpack books, film, music, media, and art to gain insight into broader meanings of social systems and ideologies through critique and critical analysis of underlying social messages about race, class, age, gender, sexuality, geography, and ability found in most texts. The aim to foster critical literacy was always present as one of the aforementioned classroom posters quoting Paulo Freire reminded: "Reading the world always precedes reading the word, and reading the word implies continually reading the world."

Second, Melissa strived to design a year-long curriculum that systematically fostered *racial literacy* (Guinier, 2004), which among other aims, coheres around goals of:

1. understanding concepts of race (e.g., racial identity, race as a social construct, colorblindness);
2. locating examples of racism in texts and in the world and examines how racism operates on varying individual, institutional, and epistemic levels; and
3. drawing on understandings of race and racism in classroom texts as a way to identify and interrupt racism in the world.

Building racial literacy in the classroom was contingent on text selection as well as committing to an antiracist pedagogy (Borsheim-Black & Sarigianides, 2019).

The year-long curriculum for the English 10 class had the overarching thematic focus on the topic of genocide. Specifically, the curriculum consisted of four eight-week units, each one building upon the last in an effort to interrogate the practices and underpinnings of genocide as it takes place in varying forms and places and toward different populations (table 3.1).

The first unit utilized the Holocaust and *Night* by Elie Wiesel as the anchor texts. The segue into the next unit centered on awareness-building around the United States' long history of genocidal campaigns against Native Peoples, which included the concept of ethnocentrism and centered Native Peoples' (hi)stories, using the #NoDAPL movement and the novel, *Wind from an*

Table 3.1 Curriculum Overview

Quarter (Eight Weeks Each)	English Ten Year-Long Curriculum: A Study of Past and Present Genocides Unit Title	Anchor Texts
1	An Introduction to Western Understandings of Genocide	• *Night* by Elie Wiesel • Holocaust
2	Reading the Word and the World: *Wind from an Enemy Sky* and #NoDAPL	• *Wind from an Enemy Sky* by D'Arcy McNickle • Indigenous-led #NoDAPL movement
3	Which Genocides Count? A Study of Genocide on the African Continent	• *What is the What* by Dave Eggers and Valentino Achak Deng • Second Sudanese civil war
4	Black Lives Matter and *To Kill a Mockingbird*	• *To Kill a Mockingbird* by Harper Lee • *13th* (documentary) • #Blacklivesmatter movement

Enemy Sky by D'Arcy McNickle, as anchor texts. The third unit cohered around the book *What Is the What* by Dave Eggers and Valentino Achak Deng and focused on genocide in the Second Sudanese civil war and the persecution of a specific African tribal population.

The fourth and final unit included *To Kill a Mockingbird* by Harper Lee as part of a larger text set—including the documentary film *13th* (DuVernay, 2016), the Black Lives Matter movement, and poems and articles by African American authors and scholars. This unit gave particular attention to systemic policies and ideologies in education, law, and society that work to create genocidal conditions of fear, violence, imprisonment, and death for African American populations in the United States.

THEORETICAL FRAMEWORK: DRAWING ON TRIBALCRIT THEORY TO CENTER NATIVE PERSPECTIVES

In rural English Education, place-based approaches are popular, yet they rarely interrogate *whose* place they are discussing and hardly ever take into consideration Native communities and Peoples. Subsequently, Melissa's curriculum is an effort to indigenize place-focused approaches in English Education.

The majority of instruction and content in mainstream schooling often fails to acknowledge Native experiences and uphold an accurate representation of contemporary identities of tribal nations and individuals, while perpetuating harmful and racist stereotypes. Melissa wanted to create a curricular space to focus on Native communities and Peoples who have been confronting physical and cultural erasure in education (and society) for a long time.

Therefore, Melissa aimed to center modern Native voices and perspectives while building nuanced understandings about how the history of colonization shapes the continued oppression and marginalization Native communities face today. In doing this, she theoretically situates this unit of study within *TribalCrit Theory* (Brayboy, 2005), which is born out of Critical Race Theory (CRT) (Delgado & Stefancic, 2001).

CRT is a framework that emerged from Critical Legal Studies and the Civil Rights movement, and it works to explain how systemic racism operates in the United States. In order to more accurately name and explain the specific challenges and oppressive experiences that Native Peoples encounter as a result of historic and current colonial systems, TribalCrit adapts fundamental understandings of CRT to frame and theorize Native-specific experiences of racism. Racism for many Native Peoples exists under the umbrella of settler colonization.

For example, in Billings, Montana, a civil rights panel hearing convened to begin the process of publicly and legally addressing the multitude of anecdotes and grievances about the discrimination Native community members continuously report in their jobs, at hospitals, in courtrooms, and in their everyday experiences in the community. One panel member, Dr. Richard Littlebear—the president of the Chief Dull Knife College in Lame Deer, Montana—provided an example of racism from his perspective by explaining that educating Montanans to recognize and disrupt the use of problematic stereotypes is a constant process and that "discrimination against Indians is still rampant in Montana and that a 'frontier mentality' is often on display at the Montana Legislature" (Kemmick, 2016).

Analyzing this example through a TribalCrit lens illuminates how specific, often historic, assumptions about Native Peoples create a racist environment rooted in the aims of colonization (e.g., positioning of Native Peoples as inferior, the enemy, and/or insignificant). Specifically, through Littlebear sharing his experience about how archaic stereotypical "frontier mentalities" about Native Peoples and their ancestral lands exists in the Montana government, his testimony demonstrates how this is a circumstance of racism that can be attributed to colonization by revealing the operating assumptions in the Montana legislature to be those of a "frontier mentality."

His recognition of contemporary Native Peoples being positioned in the state legislature within a "cowboys and Indians" framework, and the perceptions of Native homelands as extractable resources through the lens of colonial history, functions as a mechanism to exert power and control over Native communities through the laws and legislation that impacts them. These stereotypical assumptions of Native Peoples and ancestral lands are rooted in historic and current colonial understandings that strive to dismiss, marginalize, and erase Native communities as competent, complex, contemporary, sovereign communities.

As a way to further frame TribalCrit Theory, a brief overview of its nine tenets is as follows (Brayboy, 2005, pp. 429–430):

1. Colonization is endemic to society.
2. U.S. policies toward Indigenous Peoples are rooted in imperialism, White supremacy, and a desire for material gain.
3. Indigenous Peoples occupy a liminal space that accounts for both the political and the racialized natures of our identities.
4. Indigenous Peoples have a desire to obtain and forge tribal sovereignty, tribal autonomy, self-determination, and self-identification.
5. The concepts of culture, knowledge, and power take on new meaning when examined through an Indigenous lens.

6. Governmental policies and educational policies toward Indigenous Peoples are intimately linked around the problematic goal of assimilation.
7. Tribal philosophies, beliefs, customs, traditions, and visions for the future are central to understanding the lived realities of Indigenous Peoples, but they also illustrate the differences and adaptability among individuals and groups.
8. Stories are not separate from theory; they make up theory and are, therefore, real and legitimate sources of data and ways of being.
9. Theory and practice are connected in deep and explicit ways such that scholars must work toward social change.

While Melissa drew on all nine tenets over the course of the eight-week unit, the first tenet—"colonization is endemic to society"—is the pillar upon which the entire curriculum (and theory) rests. Melissa understands colonization as "European American thought, knowledge, and power structures [that] dominate present-day society in the United States" (Brayboy, 2005, p. 430).

Colonization marginalizes Native Peoples and Indigenous knowledge systems and privileges European American history, philosophy, education, medicine, literature, and culture for as Potlotek First Nation scholar, Battiste argues, "Eurocentric thinkers dismiss Indigenous knowledge in the same way they dismiss any sociopolitical cultural life they do not understand" (2002, p. 5). In this way, colonization (and consequently, racism) began existing for people indigenous to North America at the time of European contact and has continued to evolve and exist to present day.

Drawing on TribalCrit as an analytic lens, Melissa exposed her students to texts by and about Native Peoples in order to draw attention to how understandings about land and place are constructed and can be understood differently through colonial and Indigenous lenses. It was equally important to Melissa to create writing assignments, discussions, and activities that facilitated a broader understanding of *why* and *how* these communities have faced, and continue to face, pointed assimilation and erasure over the last 500 years (since European contact) and how that contributes to current conditions of and for Native Peoples.

One crucial component of the curriculum that TribalCrit supports is the task of extending students' understanding of the destructive historical truths of colonization's intent and impact on Native communities. For example, students listened to a podcast about Native Boarding Schools that intended to "Kill the Indian and Save the Man." The subsequent discussion fleshed out the purpose of assimilating Native children into non-Native settler culture as a way to eliminate Indigenous languages, ceremonies, and cultural practices (e.g., hunting, ceremonial dances, wearing long hair). In light of more complete understandings of colonization's aims, students can more readily recognize contemporary issues that reveal how colonizing practices and policies still operate to create oppressive conditions for Native communities.

In addition to more completely learning about colonization and its effects, a TribalCrit framework helped Melissa create a curriculum that focused on reconstructing representations of the unique truths of Native Peoples' survivance—survival and resistance—in the forms of Native knowledges, stories, languages, intellect, and active contributions that renounce colonially imposed narratives of tragedy and victimry (Vizenor, 2008). TribalCrit Theory helped Melissa develop a curriculum that worked against homogenous understandings of place and broaden students' perspectives of who exists in rural spaces and what relationships exist in those spaces between the people and the land.

Indigenizing, De-weaponizing, and an Anti-colonial Curriculum

As TribalCrit claims colonization has permeated every aspect of society, one increasingly popular way to address colonization in education is through a "decolonizing" approach (e.g., Au, 2009). One way to understand a decolonizing curriculum is through a decentering of colonial knowledge and the removal of colonizing ideologies that underpin curricular texts, assignments, and instruction.

However, some Indigenous scholars state that drawing on the concept of decolonization to discuss anything but the repatriation of Indigenous lands to Native nations in support of tribal sovereignty is to only further center settler colonial agendas and misunderstand decolonization (Tuck & Yang, 2012). This is an important point to hover on for the purposes of the curriculum in this chapter, since the curriculum concentrates heavily on who exists on which rural land, who "owns" the land, and who gets to decide what the land is used for. As relationships between people and place are revealed, so are differences in underlying knowledge systems and ideological understandings of place.

"Decolonization" has morphed into a term that often functions as a metonym for a wide array of social justice projects in education, therapy, law, medicine, and food systems (Chandrashekar, 2018). For example, a phrase like "decolonizing education" is often used to label pedagogies that might support degrees of inclusivity, equity, and diversity in education, but such pedagogies often fail to recognize the theft of the Native lands upon which all schooling takes place.

Furthermore, "decolonizing education" as a broad social justice project ironically often neglects to recognize the historic and contemporary effects of settler colonization on Native communities. Given these concerns around the framing and actualization of decolonizing work, Melissa's curriculum resists the label of "decolonization" as the concept has become heavily saturated in mainstream education with connotations that contradictorily have little to do with the praxis of dismantling colonizing systems in an effort to support tribal sovereignty for Native communities.

Therefore, rather than a decolonizing approach, Melisa, as a way to enact the tenets of TribalCrit Theory, considers her curricular approach *indigenizing* (as outlined earlier in the chapter), *de-weaponizing*, and *anti-colonial*.

For Melissa, a de-weaponizing curriculum means she makes curricular choices designed to center indigeneity and "resist assuming the position of cultural foot soldier for the colonizing state" (Cherry-McDaniels, 2016, p. 44). Through conscious choices Melissa made to eliminate colonially supportive, canonical texts and voices, space to indigenize the curriculum became available.

Specifically, to de-weaponize her year-long curriculum, Melissa chose to teach as few canonical texts that supported colonial knowledge systems as possible. When she was mandated to include canonical literature (i.e., *To Kill a Mockingbird*), she taught it with a critical literature pedagogical approach (Borsheim-Black et al., 2014)—meaning she utilized the text to interrogate how the author represented race, class, colonization, place, as well as how the text's presence in the curriculum itself support white supremacist ideologies, while also refocusing on marginalized perspectives that were not represented in the text (Borsheim-Black, 2015).

At the curricular intersection of the widely mis- and overused concept of decolonization, particularly by non-Natives, and the practices of indigenizing and de-weaponizing, there exists an anti-colonial curriculum of sorts—one that posits that all knowledge must serve to challenge the imposition of colonial agendas (Simmons & Dei, 2012). Additionally, an anti-colonial curriculum actively identifies contemporary colonization and works to redistribute power and disrupt the everyday and systemic colonial practices that continue to oppress Native Peoples.

As TribalCrit indicates, people are socialized into a society that supports ideals that white, western Eurocentric ways of teaching, knowing, and being are "correct" and "modern," while those of Native Peoples are often viewed as archaic, romanticized, and primitive, members of society develop colonizing mentalities that dismiss Indigenous knowledges and experiences as nonexistent, inferior, or inconsequential.

Additionally, if mainstream schools, media, and literature convey the nonexistence or solely historical presence of Native Peoples while also creating stereotypical false representations of these same peoples and cultures (e.g., mass-produced dream catchers, sports mascots of Native identities, culturally appropriative fashion), students learn to believe Native Peoples are not living, active, contributing members of the same society—further colonizing Native communities by way of exploitation, marginalization, and assimilation. A useful way of considering colonization and its negative consequences is to bear in mind that "settler colonialism is a structure, not an event" (Wolfe, 2006, p. 390).

In their article "Decolonization Is Not a Metaphor," Tuck and Yang (2012) help explain how colonialism is inscribed internally and externally in the daily lives of people who live and work in this society while continuously calling attention back to focus anti-colonizing work on the land itself. Being framed by TribalCrit allows this curriculum to explore one approach to rural English Education from Indigenous perspectives of land loss, use, connection—all of which are embedded in notions of rurality.

CURRICULUM: "READING THE WORD AND THE WORLD: *WIND FROM AN ENEMY SKY* AND #NODAPL"

By bringing together Indigenous-centric authors, perspectives, and issues with Paulo Freire's notion of reading the word (e.g., classroom texts) and the world (e.g., happenings in the world outside the classroom), Melissa's attempt at creating an indigenized English curriculum moved between classroom literacy and analysis of current events in the world outside the classroom. This indigenization included:

1. Foregrounding texts (e.g., art, film, books, articles, poetry, music) by and about Native authors, activists, poets, elders, journalists, politicians, community members, musicians, scholars, artists;
2. Making visible the differences between how the students and many Native Peoples in Montana understood place-based connections; and
3. Centering how texts, contemporary policies, and current Native experiences can help better understand the place known as Montana.

The tenth grade class this curriculum is focused on had eighteen white students, none of whom could name the twelve tribal nations who live in Montana nor locate the reservations on a map (even though the closest one is within a forty-five-minute drive away from their community). That said, for Melissa, what was paramount in educating students living in and from Montana, was teaching a curriculum that showcased how Native Peoples and tribal nations have historically shaped and contemporarily contribute to the economic, sociopolitical, environmental landscape of rural Montana.

Goals of the Curriculum

The primary overarching goal of the curriculum, "Reading the Word and the World: *Wind from an Enemy Sky* and #NoDAPL," was to create connections for (non-Native) students between historical realities of Native Peoples and their contemporary lived experiences, particularly as they relate to rurality. As an example, Melissa wanted students to be able to comprehend the relationship between federal policies that removed lands from tribal nations and how the outcomes of those policies produced material effects for Native communities today (e.g., loss of food sources and ceremonial practices as a result of removal from ancestral lands).

Furthermore, this curriculum was designed to create awareness of *contemporary* Native identities, activities, and contributions to tribal nations, the state of Montana, and the larger country; in other words, a key aim of this curriculum was to emphasize that *Native Peoples exist today*. For example, the curriculum showcases Native poets and musicians who write and sing about the rural Montana where the students lived, in some instances, less than an hour from this school.

Additional curricular goals can be framed through the anchoring Essential Understandings for Montana Indians that the Division of Indian Education in Montana's Office of Public Instruction (2019) has developed in collaboration with local tribal nations and elders. In Montana, Seven Essential Understandings of Indian Education for All (IEFA) (Montana Office of Public Instruction, 2019) exist, but for the purposes of this curriculum, Melissa primarily drew on four:

1) **Tribal Diversity.** There is great diversity among the twelve sovereign tribes of Montana in their languages, cultures, histories, and governments. Each tribe has a distinct and unique cultural heritage that contributes to modern Montana
3) **Native American traditions, ideology, and beliefs persist.** The ideologies of Native traditional beliefs and spirituality persist into modern-day life as tribal cultures, traditions, and languages are still practiced by many American Indian people and are incorporated into how tribes govern and manage their affairs. Additionally, each tribe has its own oral histories, which are as valid as written histories. These histories predate the "discovery" of North America.
4) **Reservations and Land.** Though there have been tribal peoples living successfully on the North American lands for millennia, reservations are lands that have been reserved by or for tribes for their exclusive use as permanent homelands. Some were created through treaties, while others were created by statutes and executive orders.

7) **Tribal Sovereignty.** American Indian tribal nations are inherent sovereign nations, and they possess sovereign powers, separate and independent from the federal and state governments. However, under the American legal system, the extent and breadth of self-governing powers are not the same for each tribe (Montana Office of Public Instruction, 2019).

These four Essential Understandings help facilitate the goals of the curriculum and set necessary learning benchmarks that better support IEFA requirements embedded in Montana's Common Core State Standards.

Scope and Sequence of the Curriculum

It is important to note that this unit was taught during a charged sociopolitical climate. A presidential campaign and election were occurring during this unit, and the #NoDAPL movement was at its peak, with the former occupying much more mainstream media airtime than the latter.

The curriculum contains two primary anchor texts: *Wind from an Enemy Sky*, a historical fiction novel by D'Arcy McNickle—a Montana Cree-Métis author who was adopted by the Confederated Salish Kootenai nation; and the Dakota Access Pipeline Indigenous-led nonviolent direct action movement (#NoDAPL), which was peaking in real time as this unit was being taught.

The curriculum also contained numerous supplemental texts like the song "Why" by Apsáalooke hip-hop artist Supaman, a poetry anthology comprised of Montana Native poets, and a local newspaper article titled "All of Montana is a Border Town," as well as a wide array of discussion activities employed to encourage a dialogic classroom space in order to learn through the complexities of Native histories and current realities. (See table 3.3 for more on these texts.)

Given the Indigicentric framework of the curriculum, the hallmark of its content is that the unit texts are interwoven and are not taught linearly or in isolation from one another but are worked through in a way that one concept and text leads into another and then back again, building recursive understandings. For example, five class sessions might contain two days of reading the novel, one day of reading and discussing a local newspaper article about reservation land and economy, and two days of completing writing exercises that lead to discussion about how the novel and #NoDAPL are connected *and* related to the local news story about a neighboring tribal nation. This vacillating curricular movement creates optimal opportunities for students to identify and analyze connections between historic and contemporary colonization, Native identities, and current events.

Logistically, the unit was organized into five sections embedded with activities, texts, concepts, and assessments. The middle three sections were taught in conjunction for approximately six weeks. Table 3.2 overviews each of these sections and the remainder of this portion of the chapter will explain each one in detail.

Unit Plan Section #1: Introduction to Native Studies

Given her students' lack of background knowledge in Native Studies, it was important for Melissa to provide some introductory activities to orient students. Therefore, the first two weeks of this unit began with a coordinated sequence of activities designed to introduce students to a Native landscape in Montana and familiarize them with language they would draw on for the remainder of the unit.

Learning about Tribal Nations of Montana

This unit began by introducing students to the tribal nations of Montana. Despite the fact that IEFA mandates all students across the state of Montana learn about Native histories and communities across content areas, none of the students in Melissa's tenth grade class could identify a single tribal nation in Montana by their names in their languages. Therefore, an important

Table 3.2 Unit Activities, Texts, and Assessments

Unit Section	Key Activities, Texts, Assessments
Introduction to Native Studies (~Two Weeks)	• Orientation to Montana tribal nations • Learning concept of ethnocentrism • Analysis of history textbooks • Close-reading media texts
Wind from an Enemy Sky	• Screening the film *The Place of the Falling Waters* • Analysis of maps of the Flathead Reservation • Snowball discussion activity based on excerpt from novel
#NoDAPL Movement	• Reading Treaties of Fort Laramie 1851 and 1868 • Compiling timeline and reading tribal territory maps • Four Corner argumentation activity
Linking Past and Present	Discussions of: • "CSKT Prepares for Historic Acquisition of Dam" • "All of Montana Is a Border Town" • *Birthright: Born to Poetry—A Collection of Montana Indian Poetry* • "American Indian Boarding Schools Haunt Many"
Tribal Nations of Today and Tomorrow (~1 week)	• Create an original textbook entry with specific focus

first step for this unit was to simply teach which tribal nations are present in Montana, what the nations call themselves *in their languages*, and where their current reservation lands are located.

A key aspect to highlight is the need for students to use tribal languages to say the names of the nations, which Melissa and the class practiced saying out loud together. The aim here was to produce a bit of linguistic discomfort and to push students out of their comfort zones, as staying in them was one thing that contributed to their not learning this content in the first place.

One student stated, "Ms. Horner, I feel really uncomfortable saying these tribal names. It's so awkward." To which Melissa responded, "Tribal nations have also been really uncomfortable with the English names that were imposed upon them and have thought for hundreds of years that they're so awkward too!"

Students were, by and large, nervous to say the names wrong and were uncomfortable with new consonant and vowel sounds, but increasingly gained confidence as they continued to practice pronouncing them throughout the unit. In this way, a de-weaponizing curriculum necessitates an affective and rigorous environment of instruction and learning while supporting students in an uncomfortable endeavor.

The students took a quiz—that could be retaken as many times as necessary to demonstrate proficiency—on the Anglicized and tribal language names of the nations, as well as a location component to the quiz (see figure 3.1). Additionally, with resources Melissa provided, students were invited to create group presentations outlining the history, culture, economy, and politics of each of the tribal nations.

Teaching about Ethnocentricism

A second major activity involved teaching the concept of *ethnocentrism*. Ethnocentrism is the practice of viewing another culture solely through the lens, values, and standards of one's own culture. The reasons it was important to teach this concept in this unit were twofold:

1. to begin the work of dismantling ideas of one culture or another being "right" or "wrong" or "better" or "worse," and
2. to help reframe deficits into differences, as Melissa knew cultural differences would increasingly be present as the class read the anchor novel and analyzed the #NoDAPL movement.

To teach ethnocentrism, Melissa invited students to read and discuss an anthropology article titled, "Body Ritual of the Nacirema" (Miner, 1956). In

Montana Native American Tribe and Reservation Quiz

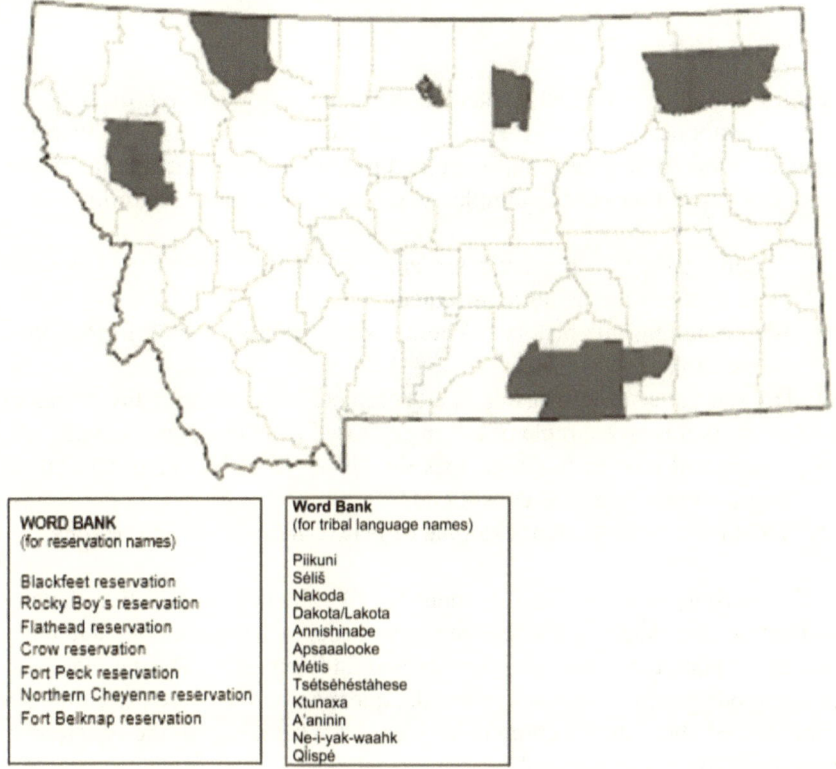

Figure 3.1 Quiz Location Component. *The map was created by Montana's Office of Public Instruction (OPI) and modified by Melissa Horner for this quiz. Reprinted with permission from Montana's OPI.*

the article, the Nacirema tribe is portrayed as a community of people with seemingly bizarre and incomprehensible cultural practices, so much so the students often critiqued and laughed at the absurdity of social and hygiene practices in this community.

While the article leads students to believe this is a removed tribal culture that was discovered by an anthropologist, close reading and discussion revealed the Nacirema are actually Americans (Nacirema spelled backward). Once the students learned this, many read back through parts of the article, gleefully stunned to realize that *they* were part of these seemingly odd cultural practices!

This activity was instrumental in making the familiar strange and teaching students to understand that people tend to view cultures outside of one's own through one's own sociocultural perspective. The aim of the activity was to illuminate that these lenses exist so that moving through the unit the students could continuously monitor how the class was viewing unfamiliar cultures through their own ethnocentric perspectives.

Analyzing History Textbooks

A third introductory activity asked students to closely analyze the school's history textbooks for Native Peoples and their perspectives and histories. Students worked in groups and were given guiding questions that the whole class discussed afterward. Examples of close-reading questions follow:

1. Which Native histories are represented in this text? What are key ways these histories are being represented?
2. Who is telling this history? Where does it seem like the information is coming from?
3. Do you get a sense that this is a "complete" story from many points of view? Is this an example of a "single story" from one perspective?
4. Where and how in this text does the "history" of Native tribal nations begin? Where and how does it end?
5. What is the most current example of Native individuals and nations?

This activity was a critical moment for illuminating how Native Peoples and nations are taught in schools and how inaccuracies and incomplete realities about Native communities are formed and cemented. During class discussion, one group of students raised the question of "Why are there only six tribes talked about in this entire history book? What about all the people who have been living in Montana?"

This inquiry represents students' increasing awareness about Native People that have lived for a long time in the place they live too, thus beginning shifts into broader understandings of rural communities. This activity was an important touchstone for the final project of this unit discussed later in this section.

Media Representations

A final introductory activity was a close reading of media representations of Native Peoples and cultures that the students worked in small groups to find and analyze (Figure 3.2). Student pairs found stereotypical examples of Native cultures and individuals in mainstream media in the forms of clothing advertisement campaigns containing non-Native models smiling and wearing feathered headdresses and standing in front of tipis with bonfires; images of numerous well-known sports mascots (e.g., Chicago Blackhawks, Washington R******s, Cleveland Indians) being circulated on sports broadcasting programming and in magazine and online articles; and in films depicting Native Peoples/tribal nations (e.g., Disney's *Pocahontas* and *Peter Pan, Dances with Wolves, Ridiculous 6).*

Students worked through critical questions to unpack detrimental media representations of Native Peoples, including the following:

- Do you see any places where the use of stereotypical imagery (war bonnet, painted face, feathers, etc.) emerges? How is this problematic?
- Are there instances where the term "Native Americans" is used as a blanket term? Why might this be an issue?
- What assumptions about Native Peoples/tribal nations emerge in the depiction?
- Are there any representations of a Native individual or tribal nation as unique and *not* part of a broad, blanket group lumping all "Native Americans" together?
- Who is the author of this representation of Native Peoples? Whose perspective is not being represented?

While finding the media examples, one student remarked, "These examples are everywhere; it's like Native American people don't even exist anymore." This student's comment speaks to the frequency and ways in which Native Peoples exist as historical figures in the imaginations of many non-Natives.

From this, the students engaged in a whole-class discussion about how these representations maintain historic (as opposed to contemporary), diminished, and deficit understandings of Native Peoples and nations. In these ways the class was able to gain clarity on the role media plays in shaping current understandings of Native People.

Unit Plan Section #2: *Wind from an Enemy Sky*

After the introductory component of this unit, the curriculum moved into analysis of two central texts—the novel, *Wind from an Enemy Sky*, by D'Arcy McNickle, and the #NoDAPL movement.

Wind from an Enemy Sky is a historical fiction novel about the Little Elk tribe on the Little Elk Reservation, whose history closely mirrors the Confederated Salish and Kootenai Tribes (CSKT) of the Flathead Reservation in rural Montana. The story takes place around the mid-1930s, when some Native people on the reservation are still living in traditional pre-colonial ways; however, the majority are transitioning into western homes and agricultural routines heavily influenced by non-Native Bureau of Indian Affairs reservation agents and the white settlers who began to populate the area.

The key tension in the text is the construction of a dam, which historically fits into the New Deal Era and the Federal Indian Policy period of Allotment and Assimilation. The dam in the book is a graphic commentary about the actual Séliš, Ksanka, and Qĺispé Dam (formerly known as the Kerr Dam) on the Flathead Reservation, and the conflict, misunderstanding, and injustice the Little Elk/CSKT experienced as a result of a dam being built on their sacred lands by settler colonists.

To develop nuanced understandings of the novel, Melissa engaged her students in a series of activities that facilitated close reading and analysis of the text while linking these understandings to occurrences beyond the text. In this way, the curriculum moved from reading the word to reading the world and back. Below are examples of three activities.

Damming Rivers

During the first few chapters of the book, since the novel is based on an actual dam and tribal nations, the class screened and discussed the film *The Place of the Falling Waters* (Bigcrane & Smith, 1990), which helped further situate the students toward the experiences of the CSKT, whose lands and waters the dam stands on, and the impact the process has had, and continues to have, on culture, lived realities, and ways of life.

Discussion questions included the following:

1. What are three new components of the Séliš and Ktunaxa history you learned?
2. Record a quote from an interview in the film that seems to address an issue important from the Séliš and Ktunaxa People.
3. What disturbed you most as you were watching this story?

Students responded with excitement about watching a documentary that included the landscape of Flathead Lake and Flathead River in northwest Montana, a place most were familiar with and that some had even visited.

Reservation Land Loss

In the second activity, students read different maps and analyzed tribal land shrinkage by year as it relates to the policies and treaties that were created (example map in figure 3.2). In looking at these maps, students learned that tribal boundaries were determined by non-Native officials at treaty time and do not accurately reflect traditional tribal territories. In the example map in figure 3.2 (Montana Office of Public Instruction: Indian, n.d.), the boundaries

Who *Has a "Place"* in Place-Based Pedagogy?   59

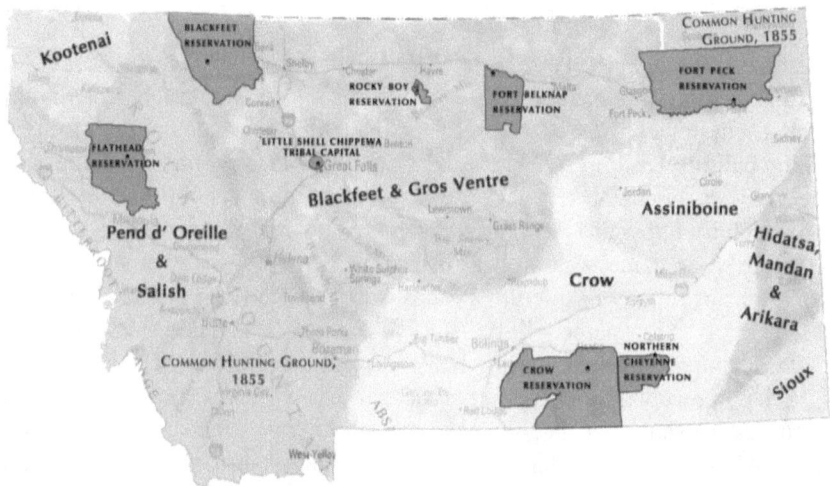

Figure 3.2 Map of Montana Tribal Territories. *Reprinted with permission from Montana's Office of Public Instruction. https://montanatribes.org*

were defined by the Fort Laramie Treaty of 1851 and the Flathead and Blackfeet Treaties of 1885.

The Flathead Reservation (known in the novel as the Little Elk Reservation) is home to three tribal nations, Séliš (Bitterroot Salish), Ktunaxa (Kootenai), and Qĺispé (Upper Pend d'Oreille). The ancestral lands of these three nations covered much of western Montana and extended into parts of Idaho, British Columbia, and Wyoming. Twenty-two million acres comprised the original territories, and the Hellgate Treaty of 1855 established the Flathead Reservation.

This activity facilitated understandings about tribal land loss so students could better contextualize the scale and rate land was taken from Native Peoples while simultaneously reading about the experiences of settler colonialism through the characters in the novel. During this activity, one student expressed, "After being home in an area for so many generations, I can't believe how fast the lands were stolen and made smaller. I bet the families were so sad. I wonder if any of the settlers and government thought this [current day] is how it would all end up?"

The activity proved to concretize tribal land loss and connect the losses to the emotional experiences portrayed in the book. Additionally, the emphasis on Native communities in these map exercises helped students better understand rurality in Montana terms of land, remoteness, formation of agrarian practices, and population density and diversity.

Close Readings and Discussions

The final activities, peppered throughout the duration of the novel, consisted of close-reading numerous passages while participating in teacher-facilitated class discussions (e.g., Snowball, Fish Bowl, Jigsaw). An example of this is a Snowball discussion used in conjunction with a reading prompt addressing one of the main character's experiences in a boarding school. For this activity, students addressed a prompt written on the board: "Please write a scenario in which your name was arbitrarily changed in some way to fit someone else's purposes." Alongside this prompt was a quote from the day's reading in the novel: "Your name will be Antoine Brown" (McNickle, 1988, p. 107).

Once students finished writing their scenario, they passed their paper to the right. Upon receiving their neighbor's paper and written scenario, they wrote responses to what their neighbor had written; this was repeated three to five times. Afterward, the students were asked to share out to the class from the paper they had in their hands at the time. When another student heard something in the current student's paper that they could build on with the content of their paper, they were the next to share aloud, and so on. This activity became more dialogic and informal after everyone had an opportunity to share.

Through this Snowball discussion, students were able to access more empathetic understandings of what it might be like to consider just one slice of boarding schools—forced name change. In doing so, this activity helped students reflect on how it might feel for them in the context of any experiences they have had with their own names and the manipulation of such a crucial part of their identities.

Through this curriculum, students think more deeply about the intersections of land, people, and rurality by reading and discussing *Wind from an Enemy Sky* through the concept of "reading the word." The paired concept "reading the world" exists in this unit with the analysis and discussion of the #NoDAPL movement, which facilitates more critical thought about rural places.

Unit Plan Section #3: #NoDAPL Movement

> It is crucial that people recognize that Standing Rock is part of an ongoing struggle against colonial violence. The Dakota Access Pipeline (#NoDAPL) is a front of struggle in a long-erased war against Native Peoples—a war that has been active since first contact and waged without interruption.
>
> Hayes, 2016, "How to talk about #NoDAPL:
> A Native perspective," *Truthout*

Paired with *Wind from an Enemy Sky*, the second central "text" in this unit is the Indigenous-led nonviolent, direct action movement against the Dakota Access Pipeline (#NoDAPL) that took place at the Oceti Sakowin camp ("Standing Rock") in rural North Dakota in 2016. At the time Melissa taught this curriculum, the Dakota Access Pipeline was a 1,172 mile long, $3.8 billion underground pipeline that was intended to carry a half-million barrels per day of hydro-fracked crude oil through four states (North Dakota, South Dakota, Iowa, and Illinois) from the Bakken oil field in North Dakota to existing infrastructure in Patoka, Illinois. The final section needed to complete the pipeline was to be installed near Cannonball, North Dakota and the Standing Rock Lakota Reservation.

The #NoDAPL movement consisted of Native and non-Native Water Protectors who formed a large camp (with smaller adjoining camps) on sacred and unceded Lakota lands in an effort to protect the Missouri River in the largest-ever Native-led coalition. During this unit, Melissa undertook two separate trips to Oceti Sakowin in North Dakota as a Water Protector in support of the movement and as a teacher-researcher who contributed her own first-hand experiences to the class curriculum as primary resource material (Horner, 2016).

As a way to cultivate understandings about the legal, social, and tribal complexities of the #NoDAPL movement, and to more deeply read *Wind from an Enemy Sky*, Melissa engaged her students in a number of curricular activities, three of which are detailed below.

Treaties

The first activity comprised a reading and analysis of the Treaties of Fort Laramie 1851 and 1868 (Fort Laramie Treaty, 1851; Fort Laramie Treaty, 1868) as the basis of learning about federal treaties, land successions, and unceded territory—all of which are critical aspects of rurality.

The concept of unceded territory means a tribal nation, the Standing Rock Lakota in this case, never signed over portions of their original lands to the U.S. government, which means the lands are still legally under ownership of the tribal nation, even though the United States is operating as though the land belongs to the federal government. This is an important curricular moment to begin shaping student understandings of land ownership in relation to the DAPL pipeline in the world and the dam in the novel.

This activity presented particular difficulties for students as they learned that the federal government is calling land theirs that was never officially bought or given to them by the tribal nation who has called it home for thousands of years. Students' reactions ranged from sympathetic, "The government has no right to be spraying those people with pepper spray for being on land that actually belongs to them!" to indignant about the Water Protectors' occupation of the land, "Even if the land used to be theirs, it hasn't been for a long time. Just like the land here in Montana. They should just leave if they don't want to get hurt."

These student responses illustrate the emotions apparent when students begin considering how land and place is conceptualized and what that might mean for Native communities, rural communities, and their own community.

Charting the Process

The second activity entailed the entire class constructing a partial historical timeline with specificity to the Standing Rock Lakota, leading up to the #NoDAPL movement, coupled with several maps (see figure 3.3) to further understand the centrality of history and land in the pipeline resistance (NYC, 2016). As a class, students were able to visually place the timeline events in order and discuss each year on the timeline, while cross-referencing the provided map in an effort to collaboratively make better sense of key federal policies as well as the evolution of the land itself.

(The central resource Melissa used for this portion of the unit was the Standing Rock Syllabus compiled by a group of Indigenous and non-Indigenous allies who are scholars and activists. This syllabus contains the map in figure 3.3, and the full syllabus can be accessed at https://nycstandswithstanding rock.wordpress.com/standingrocksyllabus/.)

Argumentation Exercise

The final activity in support of learning how to read the #NoDAPL movement as a text was a Four Corners discussion that focused on the varying perspectives of the situation. This activity was set up with a sign in each corner of the classroom. The four corners of the classroom read: Strongly Agree, Somewhat Agree, Somewhat Disagree, Strongly Disagree, with the "Strongly Agree" corner representing the perspective of the Indigenous Water Protectors at Oceti Sakowin, and "Strongly Disagree" representing the perspective of Energy Transfer Partners, the company installing the pipeline.

Melissa divided the class into four different groups and assigned each group to their "corner" of the room. Each individual student in any corner was responsible for developing a robust argument for their assigned perspective. The students worked individually, and as a whole, to provide details about and shape an argument for their assigned perspective.

For example, the "Strongly Agree" students made the argument that the installation of the pipeline was endangering the drinking water of the tribal

Oceti Sakowin Oyate Territory and Treaty Boundaries 1851-present

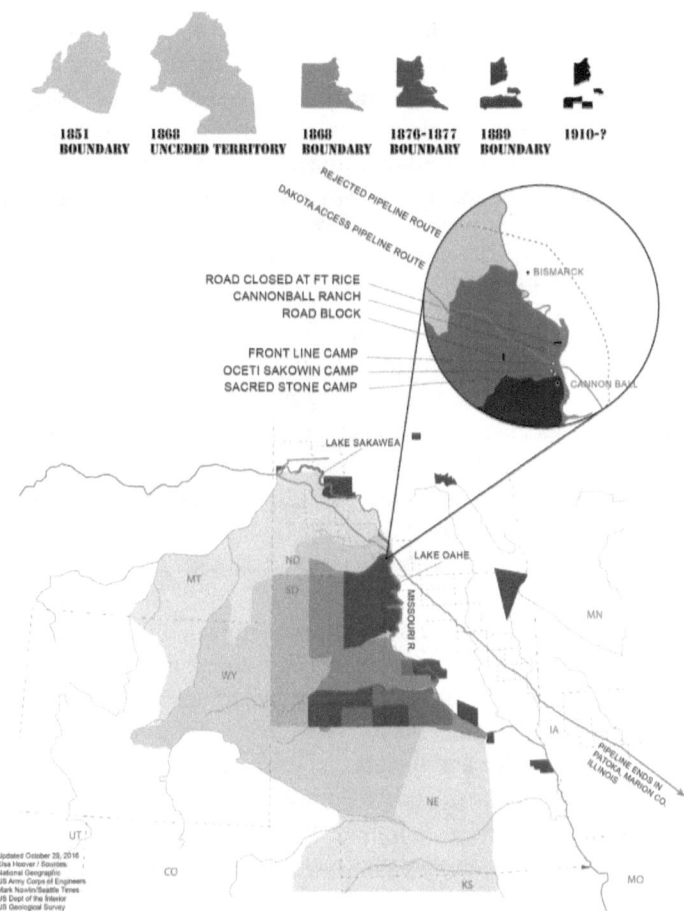

Figure 3.3 **Standing Rock Lakota Territory Boundaries.** *This map can be originally found here: https://nycstandswithstandingrock.wordpress.com/standingrocksyllabus/.*

nation and the country while infringing upon the Lakota's sacred lands, while the "Strongly Disagree" students made the argument that this pipeline was providing temporary jobs and was the safest and best way to transport the oil that the entire nation consumes.

The point of the exercise is for students in one corner to try to convince students in other corners to come to their corner. Once a student in any given corner feels compelled and convinced to move to another corner, they may do so, and then begin contributing to that corner's persuasion and argument, in an attempt to convince all classmates to move to that corner.

An important note is Melissa's assignment of students to corners. Melissa wanted students to be able to demonstrate an understanding of their designated perspective by providing evidence and details divorced from their personal opinions about the #NoDAPL movement; thus, she made an effort to counter personalization students might make in alignment to one perspective or another. The Four Corners activity was a favorite for the students, and they requested to do the activity multiple times in the unit as they gained understanding and information about what was going on at the Oceti Sakowin camp.

Linking Past and Present

Throughout the unit, Melissa interspersed a range of multimodal texts to facilitate connections between the past and the present. As *Wind from an Enemy Sky* and #NoDAPL continuously historicized the Native issues the curriculum investigates, the supplemental texts ensured Native Peoples were portrayed as contemporary people. The purpose of highlighting the relationship between the histories and current realities of Native communities was to showcase how understanding one helps facilitate a deeper understanding of the other and vice versa. This also served as a way to problematize how rurality often gets figured as historical.

To do this, Melissa wove a variety of supplemental texts before, after, and in between reading *Wind from an Enemy Sky* and analyzing #NoDAPL. The texts are represented in table 3.3 and were mostly used in discussion activities and for related writing exercises. The vehicles for discussion varied over the course of eight weeks, and included Jigsaw, Fishbowl, Snowball, Affinity Mapping, Socratic Seminar, Four Corners, Think-Pair-Share, and DICE (disturbs, interests, confuses, enlightens). Each of the texts and discussions encouraged students to consider and reconsider a variety of ways to make sense of Native experiences, land, and who exists and how in the rural places around which the majority of the texts cohere.

Unit Plan Section #4: Final Project—Tribal Nations of Today and Tomorrow

This project invited students to reflect on the introductory assignment of analyzing the school's history textbooks and then asked them to draw on all they had learned through the unit to create an original textbook entry with a

Table 3.3 Supplemental Texts

Text Title	Type of Text	Description of Text
"Why" (Supaman, 2015)	Song with music video and lyrics	Apsáalooke musician, Supaman (aka: Christian Takes Gun Parrish) who incorporates hip-hop with Apsáalooke musical instruments and dance
"CSKT Prepares for Historic Acquisition of Dam" (Tabish, 2015)	Local newspaper article	Confederated Salish and Kootenai Tribes take over ownership of the Séliš, Ksanka, and Qĺispé Dam (formerly known as the Kerr Dam) *The dam portrayed in the novel
Birthright: Born to Poetry—A Collection of Montana Indian Poetry (Susag, 2013)	Poetry anthology with accompanying videos of Native poets reading their poems	A collection of poetry from ten different Montana Native poets, along with writing activities and questions for discussion
"All of Montana Is a Border Town" (Kemmick, 2016)	Local newspaper article	A civil rights panel conducted an eight-hour hearing in Billings, MT on the subject of discrimination against Native Americans. This article shares the vivid testimony of racism experienced by Natives in the state
"American Indian Boarding Schools Haunt Many" (Bear, 2008)	NPR Podcast	For the tens of thousands of Native children who were forced into boarding schools, it's largely remembered as a time of abuse and desecration of culture
Reel Injun (Diamond et al., 2009)	Documentary	Cree filmmaker explores the detrimental portrayal of Native Americans in film
"Tempers Flare Over Deleted Cat Country Post Calling for Separate Native Tourneys" (Hudson, 2017)	Local newspaper article	Local radio host calls for segregation between White and Native Montana high school basketball tournaments
"How to talk about #NoDAPL: A Native Perspective" (Hayes, 2016)	Online blog post	Description of #NoDAPL resistance as historicized and described by an Indigenous woman
"The Great Failure of the Indians Mascot debate? Thinking of It Only as Racism" (HolyWhiteMountain, 2016)	Online article from ESPN	Blackfeet writer outlines his perspective of sports mascots that use Native identities. Specifically discusses the Cleavland Indians

(Continued)

Table 3.3 **Supplemental Texts** (*Continued*)

Text Title	Type of Text	Description of Text
"Girl has Perfect Response to Offensive Assignment to 'Dress Like an Indian'" (McCombs, 2016)	Online article from Huffington Post	An elementary student is assigned to "dress like an Indian" and she comes to school dressed as a Standing Rock Water Protector

focus on a Native person, issue, or place (see Appendix A). The entries were compiled into a classroom text representing more complete historic and contemporary representations of Native communities.

In addition to functioning as a summative assessment for the unit, this final project also established a student-written anthology for future students to read in order to learn historically accurate and contemporarily situated information about Native Peoples and tribal nations in Montana.

The students' earlier analyses of the school's history textbooks revealed glaring inconsistencies with Native perspectives of history; the omission of many details crucial to understanding current realities of land occupation and use; and representations of Native Peoples and nations that lead readers to believe Native Peoples are extinct. With this in mind, students accepted the invitation to create new textbook entries that would hopefully provide their peers with broader and deeper understandings of Native America (see student example in Appendix B).

Many students struggled with the concept of re-writing the history textbooks they'd become familiar with as an authority in their schooling experience. Melissa worked with students throughout the process to support their insecurities about possessing enough knowledge as authors to be equipped to pass along the information they had learned over the course of the unit.

It is crucial to note that at the beginning of the project one student posed the question, "If we're writing new textbook entries, and we're white, doesn't that just make us the same as all the other white people writing about Native people?" This was a welcome and critical moment in the development of the final projects, as students were asking questions about the ethics of writing about experiences and (hi)stories that are not their own, which Melissa saw as a positive sign.

In response, the class continued discussions about how the best people to share a (hi)story are the people who experienced it. And yet, the developing textbook entries had potential for valuable contribution, so the class addressed the issue of potential misrepresentation and exploitation in the individual entries by explicitly acknowledging student/writer positionality in each entry. This choice allowed for students to share valuable knowledge they had learned while also informing future readers that they were offering one perspective of a topic—a limited non-Native perspective.

Extra Credit Option

During this unit, Melissa created an extra credit opportunity whereby students could attend an open local powwow and complete a one-page write-up of what they saw, heard, tasted, smelled, and felt there. Similar to having students speak tribal languages in the classroom, this activity was designed to invite students out of their comfort zones and encourage them to engage with cultures and activities in Montana with which they were unfamiliar. In this way, this activity contributed to a de-weaponizing anti-colonizing approach by choosing to *not* offer an extra credit opportunity for students to continue to participate in activities and events that were culturally familiar to them, thus refraining from using the curriculum as a vehicle to further settler colonial dominance.

It also asks students to consider centering a day in their lives around the cultural experience of a powwow, a centuries-old Native celebration of community, culture, and place, in an anti-colonial move. Melissa recognized the powwow attendance had potential to reify stereotypes, but since students were also embedded in the class curriculum, they hopefully had opportunities to experience more complete versions of Native communities, thus countering incomplete stereotypical views of Native Peoples.

Four students attended the powwow together and wrote individual descriptions of the experience. They shared myriad reactions, including one student's nerves about attending an event "not designed for white people," another student's wonderings about how "Indian tacos" came into existence, and another's awe about the intricate beading on the regalia the dancers wore. Overall, the students' papers demonstrated a shared extension of cultural awareness by attending an event hosted by the local Native community.

Student Responses to Curriculum

Delivering this curriculum proved to be as challenging as it was rewarding. Indigenizing the English curriculum meant prioritizing Native texts and experiences in a way that unveiled painful truths of colonization and oppression that also clearly represented Native Peoples, cultures, and languages as part of who comprises, and have *always* comprised, rural places.

Making the move to center Indigeneity also necessarily meant decentering normative, dominant narratives of white rurality and place, which disrupted white students' notions of what and how they understood the land and the rural places familiar to them. Much of rural Montana operates from notions of land rooted in homesteading, ranching, agriculture, and economic development of land. These settler colonial ideas of rurality are challenged in this curriculum by original inhabitants of this land whose notions of land include cultural connection with sacred spaces.

For instance, Dave Archambault II, the Tribal Chairman of the Standing Rock Lakota during the #NoDAPL movement, explains, "The Lakota view the area near the potential construction of the Dakota Access Pipeline as both a 'sacred place' and a 'burial site,' or as both a place set aside *from* human presence and a place *of* human reverence" (Horner, 2016). Including this type of Indigenous knowledge about rural places similar to Montana (like North and South Dakota), afforded students the opportunity to begin diversifying their conceptions of rurality and land.

This disruption in the students' current understandings was met by student pushback, particularly early on in the unit as Indigenous-centric texts and perspectives decentered canonical texts and made familiar settler colonial ideologies seem strange. At times, students reacted to the curriculum with resistance and negative affect (e.g., apathy, anger), to which Melissa developed techniques to facilitate productive learning amid the emotionality and "cognitive dissonance" (Gorski, 2009) that was occurring in the classroom.

The primary way Melissa supported her students in the emotionality of learning was with the classroom practice of "meta-moments" (Petrone, 2015). This practice was introduced early in the school year, prior to the beginning of this unit, and its primary purpose was to create a space in the classroom for students to take time to explore how they felt as they learned.

In brief, "meta-moments create a space that prioritizes and normalizes the emotionality of learning, reading, and talking about concepts, events, and issues that often cause cognitive and emotional dissonance, in a way that is non-threatening. They also allow students to express real-time individual understandings, connections, and emotions that, often, there is no other space to do so in" (Horner, 2019, p. 62).

For example, during a discussion activity one student became visibly agitated when he read an article (HolyWhiteMountain, 2016) about the mascot of his favorite baseball team, the Cleveland Indians, written by a Blackfeet journalist. Other students chimed in that the mascots of their favorite teams also drew on Native identities (e.g., "Indian heads," feathers, nomenclature). At this point, over half the class became defensive about the article's claim that the use of Native identities as mascots is a racist underpinning of the systemic misunderstanding and erasure of Native Peoples and cultures.

At this time, with about ten minutes of class left, Melissa paused the class discussion and invited the students to take a meta-moment and write about two things:

1. How they were feeling in that moment—what they noticed about the emotions they were experiencing; and

2. What personal or family beliefs might be underpinning their experience of the discussion (Horner, 2019).

As the students wrote during this meta-moment in time, the emotion existing in the classroom slowly ebbed as students' papers filled.

This practice created an emotional relief valve and allowed for learning and important discussions to be paused and, more importantly, resumed again at a later time (the next class period, in this case) with more clear intrapersonal understandings of the emotions underpinning discussions. Additionally, Melissa often draws on the concept of "cognitive dissonance" to understand the emotionality of learning when students learn new information that conflicts with previous understandings (Gorski, 2009). Melissa understood the surfacing and processing of emotion while learning in the classroom as a positive sign indicative that generative unlearning and relearning was occurring amid complex topics. (See Horner, 2019, for a more robust and detailed discussion of Melissa's use of meta-moments in her curriculum.)

Through writing and discussions, students continuously shared through their feelings of surprise, confusion, and disorientation about re-understanding the rural places they thought they knew so well. For example, at the beginning of the unit one student remarked, "I never knew that because of the tribes there are at least thirteen different languages being spoken in Montana at any time." This student's newfound awareness of the many independent cultures and languages existing in her home state helped facilitate a broader, more accurate conception of the rural place she lived.

Additionally, another student wrote during a reflection exercise:

After thinking for so long that Native people are either just wearing feathers in history books or alcoholics on a reservation, but nothing in between, now knowing different examples of what Native people are doing in today's world really showed me that I didn't know anything about Native American history or that Native people where I live are teaching at colleges and being scientists every day.

This student's reflection reveals the shift in consciousness taking place around how this student is developing a broader comprehension of contemporary Native individuals and communities in the rural place she lives.

CONCLUSION

This unit ultimately provoked shifting awarenesses that created space for more complete impressions and understandings of rurality. Specifically, the students in this class had very particular conceptions of rural places, people, activities, and histories; these shifted significantly as a result of this unit. Students' previous understandings of rurality were organically rooted within settler colonial paradigms that understood rurality as white, Christian, agrarian, conservative, working middle class, and connected to concepts of homesteading, meritocracy, manifest destiny, and included cultural and economic practices involving farming and ranching.

The shifts that occurred for these students as a result of this unit happened in at least three specific ways. The first is *who*: Who is rural? Who lives in rural communities? Students hadn't had in their imaginations that the concept of rural included nonwhite people, even though they lived in a rural state whose population of Native Peoples is one of the highest per capita in the country.

A second significant shift in this unit related to rurality was the notion of *land*. The students learned that the use and understanding of land differ depending on culture, context, and history. Whereas many of these students at the beginning of this unit understood relationships to land through typical Western notions of ownership, dominion, and on the basis of economic use, this unit helped them to broaden and nuance how different people and cultures exist differently in relationship to land and a larger environmental ecology.

A third significant shift that occurred in this unit regarding the students' notions of rurality is an expanded knowledge of what happens *on* the land in rural communities. In addition to the farming, railroad work, rodeos, cross-country track, and four-wheeling happening on the land that the students were familiar with, they also learned that powwows happen on this land in neighboring towns, Indigenous-led protection of water happens in rural states, and Apsáalooke music videos are created on the land that makes of the vast plains of Montana.

Unlike the previous chapter and the next, both of which exhibit curricula that overtly names rurality as a discourse, this unit intentionally does not make rural explicit in order to decenter normative settler colonial understandings of rurality while centering Indigenous Ways of Knowing and the experiences of Native Peoples living in rural areas. As a result, this chapter takes a more inductive approach to exposing rurality as a social construct.

In this way, this unit demonstrates an approach to a Critical Rural English Pedagogy by showing who lives in rural places, how rural lands are understood, and what happens there, all without blatantly centering rurality in an attempt to destabilize rural as code for white and in an effort to naturalize Native America as an inherent part of "Rural America."

This curriculum suggests teachers drawing on place-focused pedagogies consider the Native voices and experiences that so rarely have a place in pedagogies rooted in considerations of place. Viewing Indigeneity as inherently central to rurality and place-based curriculum and instruction facilitates a place for Native Peoples and tribal nations in place-focused education. Centering Native perspectives and experiences allows students to (re)consider their own understandings of place—particularly historicized and culturally rooted understandings of land and land use—as well as how rural places are defined outside of local communities.

When place-focused pedagogies ignore the very land upon which places exist, colonizing practices of erasure and marginalization for Native populations are perpetuated. Building place-focused curriculum with a recognition that all instruction occurs on Native lands—unceded or otherwise—and is not separate from Native histories and current realities, allows for a more complete, inclusive, and honest construction of place-focused curriculum, rurality, and examination of a Critical Rural English Pedagogy.

Chapter 4

Linking Local Communities to Critical Rural English Pedagogies

Robert Petrone, Allison Wynhoff Olsen,
Elizabeth Reierson, and Catherine Dorian

Whereas the previous two chapters took deep dives into individual teachers' classrooms that exemplify a Critical Rural English Pedagogy approach, the aim of this chapter is provide multiple entry points and possibilities for developing and integrating curricula that draw on critical perspectives of rurality. In this way, this chapter strives for breadth rather than depth.

In doing so, the hope is that this chapter will stimulate many possibilities for English teachers to develop ideas that make sense for their unique rural contexts and situations.

An important rationale for this movement from depth to breadth is that there is no singular approach to a Critical Rural English Pedagogy and that, as the previous two chapters demonstrate, developing and enacting curriculum is a complex process that must take into careful consideration the particular context, the individual teacher, and, of course, the students.

To stimulate many possibilities, this chapter first takes a brief foray into the classrooms of two additional teachers—Liz Reierson and Catherine Dorian—who have, over time, made several moves in their teaching to take up CREP principles.

In Liz's section, you'll see how she mobilized the writing of poetry to both bring together curriculum and community and to create a space whereby her students could grapple with the dissonance of simultaneously celebrating and critiquing their town. Liz's curriculum raises important questions of how teachers in rural communities might engage their students in critical work without unwittingly promoting a negative attitude toward their hometown or contributing to a rural brain drain (Carr & Kefalas, 2009). Moreover, Liz's section offers a window onto the pressing questions related to how rural teachers maintain a positive status in the community at the same time that they inspire their students to constructively critique it.

In Catherine's section, you will see how she utilizes students' understandings of how small towns help shape peoples reputations to move her students into deep explorations of challenging issues related to sexuality, including slut shaming. In addition, similar to Melissa Horner's chapter, Cat's curriculum takes up issues of identity and race. Through an examination of the controversial novel, *Perma Red*, which narrates the story of Louise, a young, Native woman growing up on the Flathead Reservation, Cat's students discuss the complex intersections of race, colonization, gender, sexuality, and rurality. In this way, Cat's curriculum demonstrates how a Critical Rural English Pedagogy helps teachers respond to racial silencing within a community, as well as students' desires to have more space in school to examine and interact with one another around sensitive topics.

Following these brief peeks into Liz's and Cat's curricula, this chapter zooms out from individual classrooms to broader possible entry points and questions for consideration for English teachers interested in taking up critical work in their rural classrooms, including attention to LGBTQIA+ issues, the meth and opioid crisis, and poverty. As previously mentioned, these questions and musings are meant to inspire teachers to imagine new possibilities pertinent to their unique contexts and situations, particularly in response to and in collaboration with their students.

LIZ'S BACKGROUND AND CURRICULUM

"Small Town Contradictions"
The beauty and longing for what once was
Preserving the past and looking for a way
To call the families back and avoid
The inevitable decline
Of my
Home.
Against
This backdrop, looking
For analysis and the ability of others
To reach beyond the nostalgia to find a
Way for both rurality and criticality to exist in
Perfect dissonance

—Liz Reierson

During her freshman year in college, Liz took a discussion-based Honors Seminar class. Coming from Broadus, Montana—a rural community of 480 people in a remote part of eastern Montana—she felt a little out of place with, and even slightly intimidated by, her more urban counterparts; nonetheless, she was excited to have conversations with her peers and learn from their perspectives. When they read Aldo Leopald's *A Sand County Almanac*, a book about ecology, conservation, and a "land ethic" designed to inspire more responsible relationships between humans and the lands they inhabit, Liz was thrilled to talk about land and agriculture in a literary context. After all, she was one of the few students who had come from a small town, had experience in agriculture, and was (and is) incredibly proud of her family's legacy as cattle ranchers.

When she got to class, though, Liz found that the engaging discussion she anticipated soon became a rant session of how cows were the ruination of the environment. One student told of a hike he had taken on public land and complained about the destruction that the cattle and the rancher leasing the land caused to the creek; another classmate asserted that the cattle industry was responsible for the growing hole in the ozone layer; and still another pointed to his family and proudly stated that they do not eat beef but hunted deer and elk instead.

Liz sat in the two-hour-long class as a nineteen-year-old without the words to explain her thoughts and feelings. She knew her classmates' assessments were missing important aspects of this highly complex topic and were definitely lacking the rancher/farmer perspective. As these perspectives went unchallenged, Liz felt frustration and anger rising, and then a sense of anxiety and even fear of being unable to express her perspectives.

She worried that whatever she said would do more harm than good—that she would be mocked as backward for her defense of a way of life and a place her peers seemed to disdain. Eventually, Liz shared her experiences, noting the connection her family shared with nature every day, but she could see in her classmates' eyes an indulgent look, one that was faintly mocking—a look she would grow accustomed to but never comfortable with over the next several years at college when she shared about her hometown and perspectives as a rancher.

When she became a teacher, Liz vowed to give her students the tools to advocate for their hometowns and rural positionalities in the face of adversity and discrimination. At first, she found success engaging students and providing them with knowledge and a lexicon to think about their communities. At the same time, many of her students pushed back by pointing to myriad issues with their small town: drug abuse, poverty, problematic histories, marginalization of LGBTQIA+ people, and brain drain, just to name a few.

Though Liz recognized these same concerns, she was uncertain how to reconcile them without losing the "good" of rural communities. In the back of her mind, the fear from freshman year of college still lived—a fear that if she acknowledged these problematic issues, she would be part of the problem of reifying stereotypes of rural people. Liz then began the process of coming to terms with the fact that her advocacy was creating unconscious biases in her and leaving part of the rural story untold—even to herself—and that by refusing to acknowledge there were problems for the sake of advocacy, she was not leaving room for solutions to these problems.

In response, Liz shifted her teaching. She decided that rather than just help students celebrate their rural communities, she would invite her students to critique and articulate their experiences as rural people. Her teaching, then, focused on working with students to equip them with skills to grapple with the dissonances inherent in wanting to both celebrate and critique their hometowns.

Her teaching became about building curricula that would work to help students be visionaries to create solutions, to be the innovative business owners, to be the ambassadors of their communities even when the world around them may look down their noses at them. She also created opportunities for her students to learn and see that they were capable of affecting positive change if they were willing to be active participants in their community; as such, Liz began to take on a CREP orientation.

Liz's Community

Custer County District High School in Miles City, Montana, is part of a community that still touts itself as "The Cow Capital of the World." Contrary to the mountains for which the state of Montana is named, Miles City is a part of the eastern great plains resting along the banks of the Yellowstone River that William Clark followed on his return voyage from the west.

Colonially named for General Miles, the head of the military Fort Keogh at the edge of town, Miles City is located in the heart of Cheyenne country. Like many communities in rural Montana, Miles City is the product of a settler colonialism that displaced Indigenous Peoples to reservations, resulting in a predominately white demographic. In this case, the original inhabitants of this area, the Tsétsêhéstâhese (Northern Cheyenne), now live on the Tongue River Reservation, which is about 100 miles south of Miles City, and Miles City's population is over 90 percent white.

In many ways, Miles City exists as the center for rural communities in eastern Montana. The major basketball tournaments in the region are hosted by Miles City because its gym is large enough to host multiple schools, and it is the only community in eastern Montana that boasts both a Walmart and an Albertsons. There are about 8,000 people in town, making it quite large for eastern Montana. It is also a community made up of many small communities that could no longer support a school and are barely keeping open a post office. As a result, many people drive upward of sixty miles to come to work for large employers like the school district, Bureau of Land Management, Natural Resource Conservation Service, and the small community college.

Miles City is home to the "World Famous Bucking Horse Sale." The community comes to a standstill the third weekend in May as the town is flooded with people from all across the state to celebrate the cowboy history of this town, while imbibing excessively. In addition, every spring, Miles City opens its coffee shops and museum to host a Cowboy Poetry weekend. During this weekend, cowboys and art take center stage as published and amateur poets come together to share their experiences through poetry, performance, and the arts. As such, Miles City defies being known just through a set of agrarian stereotypes.

Liz's Curriculum: Celebrating and Critiquing a Small Town through Poetry

Liz began taking on a CREP orientation through a blurring of boundaries: she brought both place and people in and out of her classroom to position her students and rurality as embodied and in need of examination. As mentioned, Liz did not first set out to enact her curriculum through CREP; rather, her experiences (both as a rural teacher and as person who identifies and loves rural) resulted in a natural shift to add critique and provide opportunity for her students to engage in and with their communities as part of English class.

One way Liz critically examined rurality was through a poetry unit, taking on canonical and typical English content and standards and setting her students and their shared places next to published poets—one of whom was a local rancher. Liz's choice to situate her critical, placed-based work within poetry was a direct response to students' view of poetry, which most of them saw as overly academic and largely irrelevant to/for their lives as rural people. For Liz, poetry was exactly the type of literacy practice that could engender creative and innovative thinking needed to tackle the pressing issues rural people and communities face.

Liz selected poems regarding land, weather, agriculture, and relationships and encouraged students to apply their local, rural knowledge to poetry analysis; she sent students out into the community and directed them to record words they saw in town every day in order to develop found poems to describe their experiences in/of town; she invited a locally, published poet into her classroom to present his poems and work with students on their own representations of place; and she provided numerous opportunities for students to write about—and share with people beyond the classroom—their experiences of place, while (hopefully) bumping into classmates whose experiences were distinct.

Across all of these activities, Liz connected her students (as rural people) more to the discipline of English and to their communities. She also created space whereby they could work through the challenges of holding together critique and celebration and to imagine possibilities for renewal of their community. Moreover, Liz's curriculum highlights a significant aspect of CREP: providing students opportunities to create and disseminate texts into their communities.

The remainder of this section illustrates key instructional moves that Liz created so she could provide opportunities for her students to address and work through their "celebration and critique" of place. In considering these moves, readers can think about how teachers might help students (and themselves) take on the role of visionaries who may create innovations and solutions as they practice giving voice to concerns about their home town.

Poetry Analysis

To begin, Liz and her students engaged with canonical poets. First, she gave students a copy of "The Raven" by Edgar Allen Poe because many students were familiar with Poe and the mystery and suspense he tends to create. When the class discussed the third and fourth stanzas (reproduced here), students relied on their own sense of place and found the narrator's reaction to sounds in the night laughable.

> Presently my soul grew stronger; hesitating then no longer,
> "Sir," said I, "or Madam, truly your forgiveness I implore;
> But the fact is I was napping, and so gently you came rapping,
> And so faintly you came tapping, tapping at my chamber door,
> That I scarce was sure I heard you"—here I opened wide the door;—
> Darkness there and nothing more.
>
> Deep into that darkness peering, long I stood there wondering, fearing,
> Doubting, dreaming dreams no mortal ever dared to dream before;
> But the silence was unbroken, and the stillness gave no token,
> And the only word there spoken was the whispered word, "Lenore?"
> This I whispered, and an echo murmured back the word, "Lenore!"—
> Merely this and nothing more.

The students' guffawed at Poe's use of "nothing more" because in their rural experiences, darkness is never nothing: it is always filled. Students shared stories of the wind howling and racoons wrestling on the porch. Others were convinced that there was nothing more startling than coyote howls that turn into yips as the animals communicate with others of their kind. Additionally, the students took notice that the only time that there is anything akin to silence is during a soft snowfall. Living in eastern Montana, they were accustomed to the varying snow storms and used their understanding of the snow and sound to enhance their understanding of Poe's "The Raven."

Next, Liz asked students to read John Donne's "No Man is an Island" and consider issues that pertain to an agricultural background (e.g., erosion). They also read Donne's poem as a way to study language and allusions. To begin, Liz's students generated a list of local knowledge and phrases; next, they discussed what these phrases meant and noted how a few simple words could bring a whole new set of meaning to a piece. "Cowboy up" was one phrase to which students repeatedly returned. In Montana, there is the mentality that one must stand up against all odds and be incredibly tough. Additionally, because the school mascot was a cowboy, this phrase "cowboy up" was used to reference a committed member of the high school.

Students also discussed whether or not they had heard the phrase "for whom the bell tolls" outside of the poem. While most students recognized the phrase, only a few Metallica fans were able to locate the use. Liz then played several songs entitled "For Whom the Bell Tolls" and showed a recent computer commercial that ends with the tagline "Ask not for whom the bell tolls, it tolls for thee"—a reference to Donne's work. Across all of these uses, as well as their own connections, students examined how this allusion can, does, or does not apply to their community. Their most significant analysis of allusions was noted in discussions.

First, students talked about the beauty of a small town's isolation, but a community's simultaneous tendency to isolate individuals they perceive as outsiders. They noted how "one man's death diminishes me" could reference the rampant suicide rates in Montana and in a small town in America. They also considered what Donne's phrase may say about communities, and then considered how it was utilized to tell a story about a community, real or imagined. Shifting out of discussion, each student wrote a poem to address a problem and find a potential solution to it: each poem had to include an allusion to Donne's poem. These allusions, as well as others they continued to share and find, became referenced in students' own writing as well as admired for the work and thought processes of their peers.

Writing Place

In effort to further examine Miles City, Liz took her students downtown (a familiar place) and told them to "find" words on their walk (a new purpose). For example, as students passed by the pharmacy and the window sign read "razors on sale," they wrote down those words. Once their walk ended, they looked through their notes and selected the words or phrases that felt most salient. Then, students put the words or phrases together to create a "found poem" depicting their community and its values, as written and displayed across town.

With this activity, Liz attempted to make the walls between the classroom and the community "permeable" (Dyson, 2016) and she was able to engage her students in poetry production and a new way of viewing a place they knew intimately. While piecing their words together, students looked at their community with the dissonance that results from simultaneously celebrating and critiquing a place they love. As each student turned their pride and prejudices into a poem, they focused on different words, prompting the class to discuss which words were foregrounded and which were silenced—both within the found poems and the words offered downtown.

To extend ways of writing about their place, Liz assigned students to bring in a recipe; this recipe could be one that held particular meaning for them or just one that they found off the internet—regardless, this recipe would serve as their model for creation. Next, Liz asked students to create a recipe poem about Miles City. Specifically, Liz asked students to consider elements of the community—good, bad, indifferent—and share that with the class.

In another opportunity to write place, Liz asked students to write about their home in terms of food, drink, smells, and tastes. One student chose to write about home, not in terms of the food and tastes that exist, but in terms of the absence of it:

"Gone"

It's been 5 years since you had a stable family to live with.
Blame! That evil word that judges people,
Whether they deserve it or not someone will have it.
Either on their conscience or in their heart. Even children know
Or think that it is their fault.
When you wake up in the afternoon and find out that all of your electronics
Have been pawned for "rent" it hurts but you know the real reason
You get to listen to all the kids at school brag about their families,
But you get to go home and have fast food for dinner
For the 3rd night in a row.
If you are lucky you might get frozen chicken nuggets and fries for dinner.
When you woke up in the morning to try and find something,
Whether it's food or your stuff that's "missing."
It's a good feeling when you think they are sober,
Eventually you see past their lies though.
Everything becomes so fake and two faced.

Just black and white,
Just plain.
It makes you feel like you are useless and terrible,
Only after they've lost you they will begin to realize what they've done
By then it's usually too late.

When this poem was shared in class, the absent reference to electronics disappearing in favor of "rent" left peers feeling uncomfortable. This discomfort was important because without it, some students may have had difficulty recognizing the struggles faced in their own community. Liz often heard the phrase, "That may happen in a big city, but *here*_____." Though not deliberate, some students separated themselves from distressing situations in their community. By creating a space in which students shared their personal experiences, Liz found a way to demonstrate the differences that exist within a perceived monoculture.

It is easy at times to fall into assumptions of what others are experiencing, but allowing students to write their place and then share their interpretation carved out opportunity for students to recognize how diverse a small town can be—in particular, how diverse their small town is. Through a study and creation of poems, Liz's high school students realized a wider range of thinking about eastern Montana, and they engaged in discussion about why it was so important to share their voices and interpretations.

Local Poet

To further the permeability between community and classroom, Liz invited Mr. Wallace McCrae—a local, published cowboy poet who is a well-known rancher in the Miles City area—to present in class. To prepare students for his visit, Liz taught McCrae's "Urban Daughter," and tried to help students gain a glimpse into how a person in their community used poetry to process his experiences. When in the class visiting, Mr. McCrae recited several poems and showed students how rhythm can add to their performances. He also provided answers on a variety of subjects, particularly about his local experiences: "Our ranching culture is noted for being 'Hell on horses and women.'" He explained:

> Our sons are expected to take over the ranch, while our daughters are encouraged to get an education, marry a non-cowboy and get the hell away from the ranch. Our oldest daughter, Allison, did just that. While she was back for visits, I began really listening to her as she reviewed her life, past and present. She is the writer of this poem. I just put it in meter and rhyme.

Students were fascinated that someone with an agricultural background could enjoy poetry so much; however, through discussion, Mr. McCrae articulated how he shared his rurality through his poetry. It also became clear how students related to his writing because of their shared understanding of the same place.

McCrae also provided feedback on students' poetry, noting strengths and positioning the students as writers. His encouragement helped instill confidence in students' abilities—particularly as students began to write more for their final poetry book—and also provided assurance from an outside source that their varied interpretations of their community were valid.

Liz's invitation to host Mr. McCrae in her class, as well as providing opportunity for her students to be in the community as readers, writers, and poets, disrupted her students' perceptions and layered on new, critical experiences for the community to consider. In so doing, Liz began to make space for examinations and innovations rather than promoting a fixed, status-quo of schooled English in a generic place.

Finally, Liz's curriculum culminated in a poetry reading at a local coffee shop in the downtown area. This reading included an audience of community members, thus creating another opportunity to break down boundaries between the school and the town. Moreover, this situation positioned the students to share their celebrations and critiques to foster dialogue for change.

Reflections

Taking on a Critical Rural English Pedagogy orientation affords students opportunity to sit with their competing feelings: their love of and frustrations with their place. They also have opportunity to engage with others and listen to how people experience the same place (another way of bringing dissonance into their experiences). Being critical of what was occurring in Miles City was important for the students to study because it gave them a greater understanding of individuals within the community. In turn, Liz invited her students to participate in the present and future of their home place with celebrations, critiques, and innovations. And poetry became a space for them to work with the tension of doing this labor.

School buildings are often centered in rural communities and bring people together for community events, voting booths, sporting events, and music performances. What is not as common is a rural school and community connection through academics. Teachers who distribute their classroom work out into the community invite students (and others) into more lived experiences of their disciplines.

In this case, Liz asked her students to be readers and producers of text (poetry); together, they distributed ideas and creative expressions to the community in which they reside and used as the topic of their poems. By shaping critical and complex narratives of their place in poetry, students had opportunities to have their voices heard at a local level, and if carried with them, on a state and national level.

When becoming a CREP teacher in a school and community similar to Liz's, there is opportunity to celebrate and critique the community's amenities, landscapes, and people—or lack thereof. Every rural place is fraught with its own challenges, and a CREP orientation provides a way for English teachers to move forward and embrace these complexities.

Bettina Love (2019) advocates for abolitionist teaching and relies on her experiences and research in urban settings to argue for sustainable change: work that must be done in order to humanize all children, dismantle oppressive structures, and build new, just systems of education. Such a call applies to work in rural classrooms and rural communities that need to be examined. Liz's own hesitancies and ways into a CREP orientation make clear that this work is complex and emotional; simultaneously, taking place in and out of the classroom is necessary and promotes change. Together, students and teachers can open the road for dialogue of change and preservation, of conservation and innovation.

CAT'S BACKGROUND AND CURRICULUM

Cat went to the small town of Fort Benton, Montana for an interview during the last week of her undergraduate degree at Montana State University. Panicked about the looming prospect of postgraduate unemployment, she applied for one of the open English teaching jobs at the combined middle/high school, though she knew very little about the school district, the rural town, or the surrounding area.

During the interview, Cat was struck by the administration's enthusiasm to brand not only the school but also the town. After asking a series of questions to ensure that she would actually be a competent English teacher, the interviewers, noticing from her resume that she loved being in the outdoors, were sure to tell her that the nearby Missouri River offers many recreational opportunities. The town of fifteen-hundred had a yoga studio, and post-interview, administration compelled her to go downtown to purchase a coffee from the local cafe with a gift card they'd given her.

The town, with its well-kept lawns, quaint strip of gift shops, and tall cottonwoods lining the sidewalk that runs along the Missouri River, was inviting and charming. To add to the appeal, the town was only forty-five minutes from Great Falls, a small city of 58,000 people that offered regional amenities and an airport that would allow her to travel home to the Northeast. Still, Cat had ambivalence toward accepting a position in a place that was so small and far-removed from her familiar surroundings.

Prior to moving to Fort Benton, Cat was not completely ignorant of the realities of rural life. She grew up splitting her time between the suburban asphalts of central Massachusetts and the isolated, rolling hills of the Adirondacks, New York, where she lived (and is still heavily involved) in a small rural community. Growing up in that small town, her last name predisposed her to a set of expectations and occasionally to judgments that she felt unfair, but also to a general feeling of reliability on her neighbors; everyone cared for her well-being, something she neither experienced in the suburbs nor appreciated until she got older.

Due to her background, Cat assumed that she would relate to her students when it came to their relationships with rurality, yet she soon learned that while their reputational experiences were similar, they varied in an important way. While she had attended a large high school where she maintained some level of anonymity, her students had been taught in a small, rural community their entire lives and were in classes with the same group of peers since kindergarten.

Cat's students were known by everyone—teachers, administration, staff, other students—in the entire district and in the entire community. Also, whereas the high school she attended had a stable core of teachers who built their careers in the district, Cat's students were all too accustomed to the revolving door of teachers: fresh college graduates who move to Fort Benton for a year or two to build their resume and then leave.

Over the span of her first four years, Cat dug some roots into the river bottom that is Fort Benton. In some ways, she has felt accepted as a member of the community. In others, she still feels a "newcomer," and her outsider status are referenced when she teaches students about social justice issues.

While she has had supportive administration, there are often some community members who disapprove of her teaching methods. When that happens, Cat feels less a member of the community and even more judged as an outsider. Notably, it is when Cat teaches a "controversial" unit like the one mentioned in this chapter that she feels most like her students: grateful for some community support but conscious of the omnipresent sense of being on constant display.

Cat's Community

Fort Benton is an agricultural town in north central Montana and sits beneath a "bowl" of bluffs alongside a highway. The Missouri River meanders below the bluffs and through town, acting as the main attraction to tourists for quick access to fishing, camping, floating, and the Upper Missouri River Breaks, complete with an interpretive center. Tourists are invited to stroll down the riverwalk and read the signs that detail Fort Benton's importance in the "settling" of the west, highlighting the role that the geography of the area played in fostering steamboat travel and trade. Fort Benton, like most rural communities, is a product of settler colonialism that displaced the original inhabitants of the area, which in this case, is the Piikani (Blackfeet) Tribal Nation.

With a population of fewer than 1,500 people in town and about 600 living out on farms in "the country," Fort Benton fosters a sense of collective self-reliance. People who have lived and farmed in the surrounding areas for decades have close-knit ties that go back generations, yet community members are welcoming to newcomers. When Catherine first moved to Fort Benton with another first-year English teacher, they were embraced by locals and encouraged to go out on the weekends and make friends.

In fact, she learned the typicality of young female teachers being quickly introduced to single farmers as an attempt to get them to stay in town. As the district's high teacher turnover rates suggest, unless a young teacher is tied personally to the community, the temptation to leave is often driven by the stress of the high demands of the job—along with the isolation of living in a small rural community. Fort Benton does offer cultural opportunities that are able to attract younger families, such as live music at the local coffee shop, art classes offered by locals, and a new brewery.

Like many rural schools, Fort Benton High School is the backbone of the community, where locals meet to watch basketball games and students are written about in the local newspaper. Operating as both the middle and high school, Fort Benton High School serves 143 students total, grades 7–12, with many students traveling as many as 30 miles one way from surrounding farms or smaller towns. Although considered to be Class C, the smallest designation for school districts by Montana's standards, Fort Benton is known for being a "large" Class C school.

With 40 percent of students eligible for the free and reduced lunch program K-12, students come from a variety of socioeconomic backgrounds, ranging from upper middle class to below the poverty line. Demographically, 99 percent of students self-identify as white; 1 percent of students self-identify as Hispanic and Native American. Given the school's proximity to the Rocky Boy Indian Reservation (thirty-six miles away), the administration recognizes the necessity of teaching post-colonialism and Indigenous issues, and, when approached thoughtfully, Cat found that students and parents remain open-minded, which does not mean, however, that the work is not met with pushback.

The Curriculum: Reputation in a Small Town

Cat's foray into a Critical Rural English Pedagogy emerged from two motivations. The first is that Cat wanted to create a curriculum pertinent to contemporary youth issues—in this case, sexuality and its intersections with place and notions of reputation, including "slut shaming." The second is that she wanted to engage her all-white students in issues relevant to their local context related to race and nearby Native communities.

To establish this curriculum, Cat drew upon a youth lens (Petrone et al., 2015), which is an approach to textual analysis that defies traditional and deficit renderings of youth as those who are raging with hormones, have awkward social interactions, and need to be controlled. Using the youth lens afforded Cat's students the opportunity to generate more complex and accurate portrayals of youth characters in literary texts and of themselves as Montana youth.

Building on how the youth lens uses specific literary elements (e.g., theme, characterization) to facilitate analyses of how notions of youth are constructed in texts, Cat took the idea of setting and posed the following questions to help frame the curricular unit: How does living in a rural area impact how you are viewed as an adolescent? Do you believe that community members view you in ways that align with dominant discourses of adolescence/ts? Why or why not?

Another significant factor that contributed to this curriculum is that Cat developed her curriculum within the context of Montana's Indian Education for All (IEFA), which is the state's mandate that all teachers integrate Native American issues into their respective subject areas. Specifically, IEFA comprises seven "Essential Understandings," which cover everything from basic geography of each reservation to broader concepts about American Indian identity. Given the racial demographics and history of Fort Benton and the fact that Indigenous perspectives were typically absent or silenced in Cat's community, she set out to disrupt two key misconceptions: Native Americans are a monolithic people and Native Americans are members of this country's (and states') past, with no regard for contemporary life.

For this unit, Cat chose the novel, *Perma Red*, which is set in Montana and written by Debra Magpie Earling, who is a member of the Bitterroot Salish of the Confederated Salish & Kootenai Tribes who now call home the Flathead Reservation, and a faculty member in creative writing at the University of Montana. Local, controversial, and heavily banned, *Perma Red* is set in the 1940s in the town of Perma, Montana, on the Flathead Indian reservation—notably, one of the two nearest reservations to Fort Benton. *Perma Red* is a coming-of-age story that also employs several qualities of magical realism as it explores the life of one adolescent Native American girl, Louise. Louise negotiates her loss of innocence as she navigates various unhealthy romantic relationships and the systemic oppression of Native Americans. The novel touches on assimilation in Native America, adolescent sexuality, the relationships between place, reputation, and sexuality, and an overall sense of identity.

Bringing together *Perma Red* with the explicit aims of attending to the intersections of place, reputation, sexuality, and race/ism, Cat's curriculum embodies the spirit of a Critical Rural English Pedagogy by provoking students to question how notions of rurality inform various aspects of their identities, communities, and their understandings of themselves and others. The remainder of this section illustrates several instructional moves Cat made to facilitate her students' engagement with *Perma Red* and their understandings of how place informs beliefs one may have about themselves and other people—and how examining these can engender new possibilities for relating to others (and ourselves). In considering these moves, readers can imagine how they might draw upon their unique local context to similarly help students explore such issues of identity, place, and relationship building.

Listening to Students

It is important to note that this curriculum was developed over the course of several iterations and emerged as it is articulated in this chapter, in large part, due to student input. In other words, the students helped direct the aims and activities of this curriculum. In this way, Cat's section illustrates the power and possibilities of how teachers can develop meaningful and engaging curriculum when they listen to and respond thoughtfully to students.

The first time Cat taught *Perma Red*, her students' close readings shaped the unit. It became an exploration of how identity, reputation, and rurality intersect in the novel and for the readers. From their close readings, debates ranged in topics from sexual shaming and reputation to students' own experiences having their reputations and identities too often determined *for* them rather than decided *by* them because of the nature of the small, rural context in which they lived.

Students became invested in the notion of consent, as the main character, Louise, has several encounters with men which are detailed in the novel through oftentimes ambiguous language—the reader must decide whether or not the sexual interaction was consensual or not. Over time, Louise's reputation as a seductress becomes her only reputation, earning her the name "Perma Red," due to her perceived promiscuity.

Through reading this novel, Cat's seniors were better able to understand how labels, particularly in rural areas, ignore the complexities of humanity and intersect with race, gender, and socioeconomics. Because the novel takes place in a small town in Montana, many of her students expressed that it was similar to their lives in Fort Benton, Montana. And each year Cat taught this novel, students commented on the prevalence of "slut shaming" in a small town and the long-term consequences of it.

Gateway Activities

Cat began her unit with gateway activities that allowed her to discuss connections between place (rurality) and identity formation. First, she asked students to apply their close reading skills to a nonfiction article situated in Montana. Then, she provided students texts centered on Native American Studies to offer a basic understanding that they could use both in this particular unit as well as in their experiences as Montanans.

For the first text, it is important to note that Cat selected a timely article that was well-read across the state, making use of an issue being discussed across communities. One year Cat chose an article about a athletic trainer who, in another community, had sexually assaulted students in the district for decades, leaving the community reeling from the abuse and betrayal, as well as embarrassed from the negative attention. Students discussed how the community in the article was manipulated and what that might mean for student, teacher, administrator, and parent identities, let alone the impact on developing sexual identities.

With considerations of time and place in mind, Cat also helped students consider this particular event in regard to the #MeToo movement. While providing generative and disturbing triggers, students grappled with life experiences as text for analysis as well as topics for emotionally charged student-led discussion.

Second, Cat introduced basic terminologies related to Native American issues (e.g., acculturation, sovereignty), taught the periods of Federal Indian Law, and analyzed poetry written by Montana-born, Native American poets. For example, Cat and her students read and discussed M.L. Smoker's poem "Crosscurrent," which is about someone contemplating leaving her home on the Fort Peck Indian Reservation; the speaker emphasizes that there are "only four roads out," and, speaking to author James Welch, questions whether or not he ever regretted leaving home. In addition to offering a window onto a Native person's experiences, the poem also challenged students to examine their own relationship to place and rurality.

Analyzing *Perma Red*

Perma Red begins with introductions to the main character, Louise, and establishes her relationship with the boy who will work to gain control over her for the remainder of the novel. Given the intensity of the beginning, Cat started the novel with a full class analysis of the four opening sentences:

> When Louise White Elk was nine, Baptiste Yellow Knife blew a fine powder in her face and told her she would disappear. She sneezed until her nose bled, and Baptiste gave her his handkerchief. She had to lie down on the school floor

and tilt back her head and even then it wouldn't stop. She felt he had opened the river to her heart. (Earling, 2002, p. 3)

Typically, students observed the following: Baptiste is putting a curse on Louise, exhibiting dominance over her, while collecting her blood and therefore, a part of her. Students recognized that it must be some kind of love medicine, since Earling writes that Baptiste "had opened the river to her heart."

Discussing this as a whole class allowed students the opportunity to create a shared understanding that this novel would be about agency and relationships and that Baptiste embraces traditional medicine as a means of captivating Louise, a tactic that continues throughout the novel. Cat continued to have her students stay close to the text, requiring them to annotate a page or a paragraph with close reading techniques.

She then asked them to select and share a section with "beautiful language," reading these aloud to the class and talking together about how Earling composed the writing. Such conversations organically manifested into how Earling developed her characters, how she described and made use of the setting (e.g., The Flathead Reservation), and how concepts of sex and reputation coexist in place.

Passages from later in the novel provided opportunities for small group discussions, particularly because students often disagreed on their interpretations and were compelled to have healthy arguments with their classmates. After Louise's sister tragically drowns, a local white cowboy named Jules retrieves the body. Louise goes to his house and is surprised to find that the cowboy who she had previously romanticized is lonely, exhausted by life, and on the verge of losing his ranch. She finds him alone in his bedroom, and the following interaction ensues:

> The night her sister died he had crushed her with the weight of his body, his insistence, but he had not let her touch him. He had pressed his palms to her shoulders to keep her at a distance, even as she felt the heat of his legs against hers. The sharp edge of his lower rib cage had been hard against her own, unyielding, almost painful. She had to push him away to catch her breath and she realized he had been inside of her and she had not even felt his heart beating. (Earling, 2002, p. 194)

This particular passage provokes quite intense division in the classroom: a portion of the students read this interaction and believe that Louise was raped, while another portion concludes that Jules did not rob Louise of her agency and that at any point in that interaction, she still had the power to say no. These discussions, which were tense, continued through reading the novel.

Through applying what Earling writes of setting and to the world, students were better able to examine how sexuality and reputation in a rural setting go hand-in-hand, and how occasionally, the complexities of who they are as people are often reduced to their reputation. Moreover, this unit opened up ways for students to explore intersections of place, race/ism, and gender, as the novel focused on a young rural Native woman who is potentially sexually assaulted by a white rural man. Furthermore, the complexities of the novel also created an opportunity for Cat to work with her students on developing understandings of historical and contemporary issues inherent in Native-white relations, particularly within Montana.

Reflections

Centered around a Native-authored, Montana-based novel, Cat's unit illustrates how one rural teacher enacted her intent to help her students consider how their local contexts help them shape their reputations: both of themselves and others. One challenge of teaching and living rural is navigating the microcosm of personalities, intricacies, and nuances of the community; while students are comfortable with one another, they too are navigating their identities, which are oftentimes imposed upon them by the community before they themselves can figure out who they are. Last names and siblings can act as determinants of one's reputation and therefore, potential success and failures. When students make mistakes in the community, adult members, including teachers, are made aware. The same is true, incidentally, the other way.

Cat used *Perma Red* to discuss rurality, as well as relate to and layer in Native American issues and broader Montana events. As such, Cat's curriculum helped students understand how their rural context was shaping their sense of self; she also leaned into dissonant and often, biased perspectives of Native Americans who are typically silenced in Fort Benton. Given Cat's willingness to make space for controversial, personal topics her students wanted to discuss, she not only stretched her students but made herself vulnerable. With both, she took on a CREP orientation because she made space to sit in the discomfort, or dissonance, and write and talk through it with her students—as the discipline of English promotes.

We recognize that all of this work—from textual choices to opening up issues of race, to sanctioning class time for students to discuss sexuality—is bold. And it didn't go unnoticed: a few parents wondered about Cat's values and religious beliefs. What may be most critical to bear in mind for this book is how Cat followed her students' lead and guided them on a path that she knew would garner attention from parents and other community members. In so doing, she asserted how ready her rural students were for complex issues that take their rural living into consideration and critique.

As is the case with both Cat and Melissa, building curriculum that emphasizes Native perspectives and issues necessitates a commitment to learning Native content, as it is not often taught in schools and/or as part of teacher education. Often, attempting to integrate Native texts and perspectives into the English curriculum can be met with resistance in some conservative, white rural communities that have histories and identities rooted in the displacement of Indigenous Peoples. Thus, we recommend that teachers interested in taking up a Critical Rural English Pedagogy educate themselves and investigate initiatives pertinent to their communities and states. Finding footing in ongoing or broader initiatives helps to bolster what can feel like an isolated teacher's effort to raise consciousness and do vulnerable work.

ADDITIONAL ENTRY POINTS FOR DEVELOPING A CRITICAL RURAL ENGLISH PEDAGOGY

These brief classroom illustrations from both Cat and Liz offer glimpses into another two English classes where teachers and students grapple with the complexities, challenges, and joys of taking a critical perspective on rurality with rural students. The four rural teachers featured in this book inspire multiple possibilities for developing pedagogical practices designed to facilitate critical analysis (of rurality as a concept) and activism (to mitigate the marginalization of rural people and communities).

Recognizing that the possibilities for a Critical Rural English Pedagogy far outnumber the incredible work of the four teachers and students highlighted in this book, the remainder of this chapter creates space for other issues that rural teachers, students, and community members have articulated throughout our research as pressing concerns. We offer them here as "discussion starters" or potential "entry points" that English teachers might mobilize and adapt in their movement toward a CREP.

Getting to Know the Land beneath Your School

One of the lessons learned from Melissa Horner's chapter and echoed in Catherine's curriculum in this chapter (and will be further discussed in the next chapter) is that notions of place need to be nuanced and deepened. One potential project, that teachers might engage their students with could be investigating the literal land their school sits upon.

Which tribal nations, for example, call(ed) that area home? Is the land (un)ceded? What treaties are pertinent? Are there current land disputes or court cases? Such an inquiry offers powerful possibilities for engaging students in not only learning about the history of their community but potential social action; for example, students may develop a plaque or some other way to commemorate the original inhabitants of the land that is respectful. (Melissa's chapter has several resources that could provide places to start to do this work.)

Related, as Melissa's chapter demonstrates, this inquiry could easily move beyond historicized notions of Native Peoples to include understandings of tribal nations *now*, which may be particularly generative for students whose schools are on and/or near reservations. Furthermore, such a project could provide generative interdisciplinary possibilities, as it inherently involves history, social studies, the English Language Arts, and potentially other disciplines. Students could research past treaties as well as current issues and policies, including school mascots.

What Are the Ruralities?

One of the lessons learned from Alli Behrens' chapter is that rural itself is discursively constructed and not a singular or essentialized entity. Therefore, another approach might be emphasizing how the very idea of rural is a social construct and that the experiences, perspectives, and demographics of rural people are diverse and intersect with myriad factors, including race, history, and geography—something illustrated in both Liz and Catherine's curricula.

In other words, such inquiry could lead students to understand that there is no singular, monolithic sense of rural and that it might be better to think of rural*ities*. For instance, rural in eastern Montana looks and feels very different than rural in Western Montana, let alone the Bootheel of Missouri, a holler in Appalachia, or a border town in Texas.

Alli's chapter effectively demonstrates how a curriculum can help students make sense of how rural as a concept is discursively developed, reified, and challenged, particularly through texts such as literature and media. In these ways, curriculum can help challenge the "single-story" (Adichie, 2009) of rurality. Liz's curricula, too, offers a glimpse into how, even within a single community, rural experiences of can differ quite radically depending upon a students' location as being from "the country" or "in town," issues of socioeconomics, or, as discussed later in this section, one's sexual orientation.

Critiquing Rurality

One of the lessons learned from Liz's curriculum is how vital it is for rural students to be engaged in both celebration *and* critique of their local community. Advocates of social justice and/or critical English Education within rural contexts (including ourselves) often position rural communities within a broader discourse of equity and social justice vis-à-vis suburban and urban contexts and issues, including addressing aspects of access, disparities, and metro-centrism/normativity.

While this work needs to continue, it is also important that the field of English Education examine how rural spaces and places have functioned historically and sometimes continue to operate as mechanisms of segregation, white supremacy, and marginalization for some of its members—something Catherine's curriculum explicitly addresses and a topic that will be given more attention in the next chapter. Also, Liz's curriculum demonstrates that there can be great value to engaging students in sustained critique of their own communities.

Melissa's chapter also demonstrates the affordances of taking on an often-silenced notion of place (whose *land* and *place* is this?), particularly when teachers provide opportunities for students to learn more information and produce updated, culturally accurate texts. What might it look like, for example, for critical English educators within rural contexts to both help students understand how rural writ large is often marginalized within broader cultural discourses *and* that rural communities themselves are sometimes marginalizing and problematic spaces and places—not just historically but also currently—for some people?

Infusing the Curriculum with Rural Representations

Another entry point into developing a Critical Rural English Pedagogy is through text selection. Rural (and suburban and urban) students need to see rural characters in texts, they need to read texts written by rural authors, and they need to read informational texts about rural issues. Catherine's and Liz's curriculum offer great examples of this, as Liz included a local poet and Catherine's central text was local author. These examples, as well as Alli's and Melissa's curriculum, demonstrate the importance of listening to students and seeking out local resources (including people).

Beyond simply accessing such resources, students need to engage them with a critical lens that examines their renderings of rural (i.e., Alli's Critical Rural Perspective). Related, given the tenets of the curricula shared and the book in general, particularly the perspectives that will be shared in chapter 5, it is important to be mindful of integrating texts that provide a broad range of experiences of rural people, places, and geographic areas. In other words, just selecting texts that have rural characters does not guarantee adequate representations of the diverse demographics and experiences of rural communities.

From this starting place, teachers might develop critical media literacy units that explicitly address depictions of rurality. It could even be generative to engage students in analysis of traditional canonical works, examining the texts for how rurality is included (or not). And, drawing on the lessons learned from Liz to further promote the connections and use of CREP, teachers can provide opportunities for students to produce *and* distribute texts within their classroom and communities and beyond.

Addressing "Controversial" Topics and Issues

Given that a CREP orientation asks teachers to think about how rurality is constructed and how rural students and teachers engage with one another and their place, we recognize that the topics raised in the four featured classrooms take on some key issues and leave others unexamined. We also note that this lack is not to be read as a lack in these four teachers; rather, it is an acknowledgement that the curricula shared are not exhaustive and that the pressing rural issues are quite extensive.

Throughout our interviews and interactions with rural English teachers, community members, and students, we have noticed that there are a set of issues that rural people consistently point to as pressing, though often challenging to discuss or meaningfully attend to; in fact, many rural teachers have expressed concerns that broaching some of these topics in their classrooms could get them into trouble—officially or unofficially. To that end, in the final chapter of this book, we explore some of the ways teachers might manage some of these challenges.

In the remainder of this chapter, though, we focus on articulating, albeit briefly, some of the issues the people with whom we have interacted have shared with us as vital to address in rural communities. It is important to note that we do so somewhat cautiously as, aware of the deficit-laden prevailing dominant narrative of rural, we do not want to contribute to or recapitulate this.

However, it would be irresponsible for us to not give voice to the concerns expressed to us and/or to try and buff out the complexities and contradictions inherent in rural spaces and places. In fact, we see this list as a set of issues and concerns that an entire English curriculum oriented toward a Critical Rural English Pedagogy could develop. Again, it is important to note that this list is not exhaustive, and our purpose in articulating the issues is to raise awareness and pose some questions to stimulate possibilities for developing curricula, not prescribe solutions.

LGBTQIA+ Issues

One key concern many rural teachers point to is a tendency for rural communities to have conservative, fixed perspectives about gender binaries and people who identify as LGBTQIA+, thus creating inhospitable circumstances for some students. Teachers expressed that while this marginalization may be occurring in other spaces, in rural communities there is less access to resources, including other LGBTQIA+ people. Moreover, current research indicates that while LGBTQIA+ youth have higher rates of suicide, homelessness, mental health issues compared to heteronormative youth, LGBTQIA+ youth from/in rural contexts often fare even worse (Paceley, 2018).

In this sense, there is a profound need to create opportunities within rural communities to critically examine and discuss LGBTQIA+ issues, and we imagine a Critical Rural English Pedagogy as one way to do this. For example, how might English teachers and media specialists make resources, including within classroom libraries, available for youth, even if not part of the official curriculum? Special attention here can be given to texts that explicitly focus on LGBTQIA+ issues as they intersect with rurality (e.g., *The Miseducation of Cameron Post*).

More significantly, what might an official curriculum look like that explores LGBTQIA+ issues? How might it be part of a unit on media or literary study or the research paper? What opportunities might there be for interdisciplinary curriculum to be developed? For connections across classroom and community? For even broader social activism to be part of the official curriculum?

Higher Education

Teachers also indicate a tenuous relationship between (higher) education and rural communities. Teachers note that some community members, including parents of students, have ambivalence about their child being prepared for and attending a university. On the one hand, they, of course, want their children to be educated well and set up for success in the world. On the other hand, they sometimes express apprehension about their child being prepared to leave them, their community, and their ways of life.

Rural brain drain (Carr & Kefalas, 2009) is a concern, as youth leave for college and parents and business owners wonder if they will return. In general, the mostly unilateral direction of education was clear—one became educated in a rural community to leave the rural community. People also worry about youth returning to visit and being changed, espousing value-laden judgments of their rural communities' practices and beliefs. Alongside this and tenuous relationship with higher education is often an underlying question or concern, even if it is not articulated overtly: Whose knowledge is valued in school spaces and how do schools make use of (or not) rural communities' funds of knowledge? Who are the experts?

Because of how schools tend to privilege non-rural knowledges, ironically, many rural communities actually feel alienated by schools, even though schools often function as the hub of rural communities. How then, might a Critical Rural English Pedagogy turn this tension into curriculum that brings together classroom and community to facilitate generative discussion about this topic? Would it be possible, for example, to bring community members together into dialogue with youth who are currently attending university or recently graduated—and who do plan or do not plan return to the community to live?

What might it look like to explicitly teach students about the notion of a rural brain drain? What literary and nonfiction texts might be generative to bring into the English classroom to explore this topic? How does this issue have particular significance for Native rural communities, where youth leaving for university is not only an issue of brain drain but also related to issues of assimilation and colonization? How does this issue interplay with other rural BIPOC communities?

Drug Addiction

Teachers also voiced concerns about drug abuse, particularly the prevalence of alcohol consumption and a growing increase in methamphetamines and opioids—for both their students and adults (often parents) in the community. While drug abuse is not just a rural issue, though particular forms of drug abuse are more prevalent in rural communities (Macy, 2018), the lack of support and healthcare in remote areas present particular problems and compounds concerns. Teachers also articulated that in small, rural communities, privacy and anonymity were difficult to come by; thereby, anyone seeking help or treatment would likely be visible in ways that could be damaging for/to them and their families.

In addition to creating challenging circumstances in the community and the school, rural English teachers wondered what they could do in their curriculum to bring awareness to these issues and even attempt to mitigate their effects. In drawing inspiration from these teachers, we wonder, too, how a Critical Rural English Pedagogy might engender curriculum that focuses on this pressing issue.

How might, for example, Beth Macy's nonfiction book, *Dopesick: Dealers, Doctors, and the Drug Company that Addicted America*, which offers an exploration into the current opioid crisis particularly related to rural people and communities, be used within a secondary English class to attend to both issues of drug addiction in rural contexts and English Language Arts Standards? In what ways might an English curriculum with this focus bring curriculum and community together? In what ways might a Critical Rural

English Pedagogy that focuses on this topic affect social change within the local rural community?

Poverty

Nearly every teacher interviewed discussed the poverty that touches the communities they teach in and the lives of many of their students. Many talked about statistics of free and reduced meals, as well as the small refrigerators filled with snacks and drinks they stock on their own dimes and keep for students in need. Additionally, many teachers discussed the vast wealth disparities present in their rural contexts, as well as how these mirror disparities in academic outcomes, as well as fuel classism and tensions, at times, among students across differing socioeconomic statuses.

In what ways, might English teachers build curricula to raise awareness about not just the surface level manifestations of poverty but the underlying structural issues related to local and global economies, particularly related to agriculture and natural resources (e.g., mining, forestry) that are often integral to rural communities? What texts, including memoir and other nonfiction (as well as literary), might be used to facilitate understandings of these complex issues?

For example, how might Sarah Smarsh's memoir, *Heartland: A Memoir of Working Hard and Being Broke in the Richest Country on Earth* be studied for not only its exploration of rurality and poverty but also as a mentor text to inspire rural students to write and share their stories? And, like previously mentioned, how might such curricula bring together community and classroom in ways that might promote improved economics within the local context and perhaps even healing?

Agriculture and Food Oppression

One of the ironies several teachers pointed out was that, though most rural places are intimately connected to the land and practices such as agriculture, rural people often have challenges accessing healthy food, and in some instances, rural communities might be experiencing food oppression or apartheid (formerly described as "food deserts"). This situation seems ripe for a Critical Rural English Pedagogy to promote curricula whereby students are reading about food systems, dialoguing with community members—from grocery store owners to farmers—about their practices, to researching the history and economics of agriculture and food production in the United States, to creating texts to share in their communities and perhaps beyond.

It is important to note, too, that, given our attention in the book to Native communities, issues of food sovereignty and self-determination could be particularly generative for rural students, especially those on reservations. For

Native students studying these issues could also engender deeper understandings and potential for activism regarding tribal and educational sovereignty. For non-Native rural students, examining issues of food sovereignty can help counter food oppression that exists in some rural areas and facilitate a broader understanding of neighboring Native communities. Furthermore, such a curriculum can link to issues of race/ism, as will be explored in the next chapter.

Though potential resources abound, including documentaries (e.g., *Bad Sugar*) and nonfiction books, we might suggest Michael Pollan's *In Defense of Food* and/or *The Omnivore's Dilemma* as good starting points in terms of book-length texts. From an English Language Arts perspective, one approach to this topic could be an emphasis on the rhetoric of food systems. Students can engage with this topic while also developing their understandings of and skills in rhetorical analysis and argumentation—both of which are crucial components of the current English Language Arts Standards.

In these ways, such a manifestation of a Critical Rural English Pedagogy would bring together local concerns and broader systemic factors contributing to local concerns; traditional academic standards and critical literacies; and curriculum and community with the aim of promoting deeper understandings and positive change.

Race and Race/ism

Teachers expressed concerns regarding issues of race and racism within their rural communities. Teachers who taught in predominately white contexts shared how the conversations they could broker in class were often limited, and even at times, included quite ignorant and racist comments from students. Teachers in communities with more racially-diverse demographics. Teachers spoke of existing tensions and difficulties in working through them with students. Nearly every teacher interviewed shared a commitment to infuse their curriculum with issues of race but were challenged with how to do so effectively.

Recognizing the challenges and importance of this particular topic—as well as how the school subject English, particularly through the study of literature, often "evokes" race whether one intends to teach about it or not (Borsheim-Black, 2015)—we have designated the entire next chapter to the intersection of rurality and race/ism. The chapter zooms out from individual classrooms to offer broad understandings of the complexities of race/ism and rurality. Though not focused on pedagogical practices, the next chapter is designed to stimulate possibilities for how rural English teachers might move toward a Critical Rural English Pedagogy with a particular focus on race.

Part III

MOVING FORWARD

Chapter 5

Re-Thinking Race/ism and Rurality in English Education

Melissa Horner, Robert Petrone, and Allison Wynhoff Olsen

When I think of rural America I think of my hometown of Tifton, Georgia. I think of my grandmother's town. I think of rural America as Black, Latinx, and Indigenous. Our failure to acknowledge this diversity has the potential to create serious gaps in our policy solutions which leaves people of color in rural communities behind.

—Alisa Valentin, 2018, "Why Rural Communities of Color are Left Behind: A Call for Intersectional Demographic Broadband Data"

In defining rural white America as rural America, pundits, academics and lawmakers are perpetuating an incomplete and simplistic story about the many people who make up rural America and what they want and need. Ironically, this story—so often told by liberals trying to explain the recent rise in undisguised nativism and xenophobia—serves to re-privilege whiteness. Whiteness is assumed; other races are shoved even further to the margins.

—Mara Casey Tieken, 2017, "There's a big part of rural America that everyone's ignoring"

Thus far, this book has taken deep dives into rural English classrooms to explore what a Critical Rural English Pedagogy might look like in different contexts. With the exception of Melissa Horner's chapter and the section on Catherine Dorian's curriculum, both of which look at how notions of rurality get complicated through indigenizing an English curriculum, this book has not given much overt attention to intersectionality (Crenshaw, 1991) when it comes to rural identities and pedagogical possibilities related to issues of race.

This is particularly noteworthy given Robert and Allison's racial positionalities as white scholars, especially as we consider—as we will discuss throughout this chapter—that so much of rural scholarship takes whiteness for granted and is carried out by white scholars who focus on white people and communities. Therefore, in this chapter, we zoom out from individual classrooms and pedagogical practices in order to draw attention to and work against these dominant racialized understandings of rurality. Our hope is that, though this chapter does not focus on classroom practices, it will engender possibilities for developing and enacting curricula in rural contexts that address various intersectional identities.

In academic research, popular culture, and mainstream media, rural often gets coded as "white"—perhaps none sharper than leading up to and in the wake of the presidential election of Donald J. Trump in 2016. This whitewashing of rurality tends to marginalize, or worse, render invisible BIPOC communities in rural contexts, particularly when it comes to discussions about rural education. Even in academic scholarship focused on rural communities, race is often neglected in favor of other identity markers, especially class and socioeconomics, and whiteness is typically assumed (Tieken, 2015).

And while it is true that the majority of people who live in rural contexts are, in fact, white, as educational scholar Mara Casey Tiekan (2017) explains, "there's another rural America that exists beyond this rural white America." Statistically, approximately 20 percent of rural residents are people of color. Of these more than ten million people, about 40 percent are African American, 35 percent are nonwhite Hispanic, and 25 percent are Native American, Asian, Pacific Islander or multiracial. See Figure 5.1 for a visualization of this breakdown.

Moreover, racial demographics are increasingly shifting in rural communities, as people of color are accounting for larger percentages of rural populations (HAC, 2012). For example, whereas about 85 percent of the rural population was white in 1990, that number declined to 82 percent in 2000, and a decade later, in 2010, it declined again to 78 percent (Kirschner et al., 2006; HAC, 2012). Furthermore, this trend is expected to continue as rural areas continue to see an increase in Latinx[1] immigration (Sierk, 2017). Given these ruralities, rural contexts necessitate increased attention to issues of race by educational research, policy, and practice.

This chapter gives explicit attention to the intersections of race and rurality with the intent of troubling prevailing taken-for-granted assumptions in rural English Education. Specifically, while much of rural English Education emphasizes place-focused approaches, little consideration tends to be given to critical questions of "whose" place such approaches emphasize. Too often, whiteness is the default.

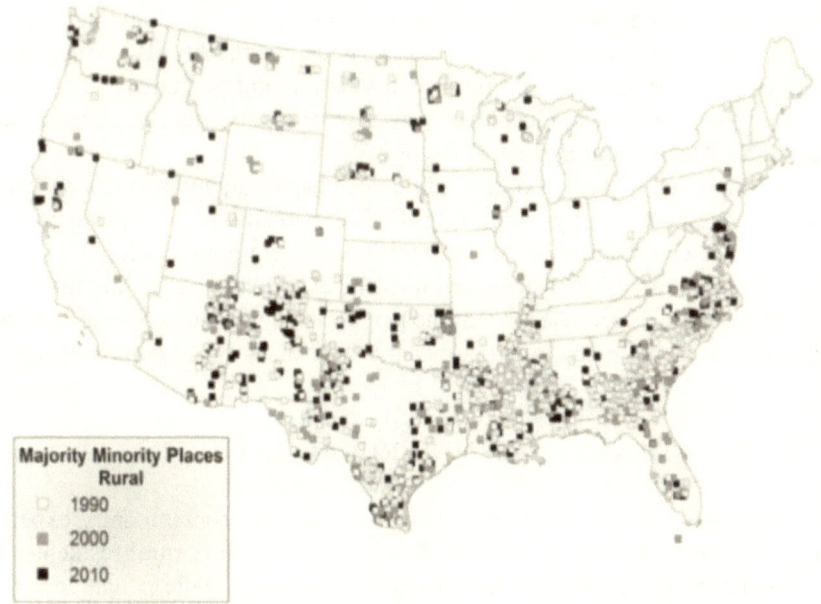

Figure 5.1 Map of Racial Demographics. *This map was originally published in the following: Lichter, D. T. (2012). Immigration and the new racial diversity in rural America. Rural Sociology, 77(1), 3–35. It is reprinted with the author's permission.*

This is particularly significant as virtually all rural places in the United States are laden with historical and current issues of race/ism embedded in legacies of settler colonialism. For example, all notions of rural in the United States are predicated upon the forced removal and resettlement of Native people from rural landscapes, the enslavement of people from Africa to work agricultural fields in various rural areas across the United States, and the drawing of boundaries and borders to exclude Latinx people from American citizenship.

Toward these aims, this chapter offers perspectives on the historical and contemporary experiences and perspectives of Native American, African American, and Latinx people living and working in rural contexts across the United States. Though many other racial demographic groups live in rural spaces, these three comprise the majority of racially-minoritized groups in rural spaces and as such offer unique ways of understanding rurality and race, particularly within the context of English Education.

By centering these groups of rural residents, this chapter attempts to interrupt dominant narratives of rurality as white spaces and places, and in doing so, helps illuminate the complex contours of both rural communities and "rurality" as a concept that exists within the American cultural imagination.

In this way, this chapter is less about particular classroom strategies and more about expanding understandings of the very idea of rurality. By bringing to light complex perspectives on rurality, teachers might be better equipped to develop pedagogical practices that work toward equity and social justice as part of a Critical Rural English Pedagogy.

It is important to note, too, that while this chapter attempts to trouble prevailing notions of rurality within English Educational scholarship, we recognize that the communities grouped in this chapter are not monolithic and are comprised of individuals whose identities and experiences vary. Additionally, it is important to acknowledge that the perspectives offered here, particularly historical ones, are partial and not meant to be exhaustive or comprehensive.

DENATURALIZING RURAL AS WHITE

Before moving into a discussion of the histories and contemporary experiences of Native American, African American, and Latinx rural residents, it is essential to recognize that the current dominance of white people in rural communities across the United States is not natural or inevitable. White people are not more innately drawn to rurality as Black, Indigenous, and People of Color are not innately averse to rurality.

Rather, the overwhelming preponderance of white populations in rural spaces is the result of designed, systematic historical processes embedded in racism, capitalism, colonization, and genocide that have created deep racial segregation. In other words, current racial residential patterns are legacies of slavery, colonization, and genocide (Lichter, 2012) that have pushed many BIPOC folks out of rural spaces and onto remote reservations and/or into urban spaces.

In these ways, rurality has, since its development in the United States, been a key site to uphold settler colonialist and white supremacist logics and practices. Part of the aim of this chapter, then, is to expose some of the mechanisms whereby whiteness and white supremacy operates in rendering understandings of—as well as policies, practices, and programs for—rural communities and people.

In addition, it is important to note that rural places that have *not* been completely transformed to all-white spaces are often ignored in mainstream media and research. For example, Drum (2017) explains how the mainstream media skews perception of "rural" America by only representing particular geographic areas of the country that are primarily white. For instance, he explains how media reports on rural America mainly focus on states like Ohio, Indiana, or Pennsylvania. In this way, he argues that "rural" actually "means the Midwest and the Rust Belt" (Drum, 2017). For instance, in figure 5.2, the shaded area is what most commonly gets reported as "rural" in the media.

This process of representing rural as white then becomes "self-perpetuating" as this coverage promotes a vision for its audience whereby they "largely see rural America as White, and that in turn means that news items about non-White areas usually end up getting coded as something else: In the Deep South they become 'race and the lingering effects of slavery' stories, and in the Southwest they become 'Hispanic immigration and the changing demographics of America' stories" (Drum, 2017).

In this way, "rural America" maintains its status in the imaginations and discourses of mainstream American media, politics, and education as a singularly white-populated space where rural racialized minorities are ignored

Figure 5.2 Representations of Rural in the Media. *This map was originally published in the Housing Assistance Council (HAC) (2012). Rural Research Briefs: "Race and Ethnicity in Rural America." Washington, DC: The Housing Assistance Council. This map is reprinted from how it appeared in the following article: Drum, K. (2017, April 24). How white is "rural America"? Mother Jones. This map is reprinted with permission from both the author and the Housing Assistance Council.*

or entirely forgotten or understood outside of the purview of rural. Thus, rurality is continuously promulgated as white despite the fact that Black, Indigenous, and People of Color live—and have for generations, and in the case of Indigenous Peoples, since time immemorial—in rural places.

In these ways, rural has both *been made white* by historical processes linked with genocide, colonization, and capitalism, *and is kept white now* within the American consciousness and cultural imagination by continued processes of erasure and racism. Thus, Black, Indigenous, and People of Color in rural spaces are doubly disadvantaged given that rurality is an already marginalized demographic (as discussed in chapter 1), particularly in relation to issues of access and representation, as well as metrocentricism and urbanormativity (Thomas et al., 2011).

Therefore, by illuminating historical and sociological understandings regarding Native, African American, and Latinx communities in rural America, this chapter resists traditional, dominant discussions of (white) rurality. Instead, it helps to promote more comprehensive and honest views of rurality as cosmopolitan, racially diverse, and complex spaces and places. In doing so, it also promotes a new sense of possibilities for a Critical Rural English Pedagogy—one that works for and on behalf of *all* rural students and communities.

THE INTERSECTIONS OF RURALITY AND NATIVE AMERICAN COMMUNITIES

The day the earth wept,
a quiet wind covered the lands weeping softly like an elderly woman,
shawl over bowed head.
We all heard, remember? We were all there. Our ancestral blood remembers...
Lois Red Elk (Dakota/Lakota), 2011, "Our Blood Remembers"

But where could we travel and not long for the ache of wind blowing over open land? And how long could we have held ourselves back, away from our need to feel claimed by a place we can only, with our limited tongue, call home.

M.L. Smoker (Assiniboine), 2005, "Birthright"

It is troubling that any conversations about rural America could and would start without (first) acknowledging the Indigenous Peoples who have lived and continue to live in rural spaces and places across what is colonially known as "The United States." Indigenous people have existed on this land—and continue to do so—with cultures, languages, families, knowledge systems, and economies long before "rural" was even a term used to designate such spaces and places.

Hundreds of Indian Reservations, Alaskan Native Villages, Pueblos, Tribal Statistical Areas, and Rancherias comprise rural landscapes and small towns across the United States, and while only 2 percent of the overall rural population self-identify as Native people, the majority (54 percent) of Natives live in rural areas—with 68 percent of Natives living on or near reservations or tribal lands (First Nations Development Institute, 2017).

Specifically, "large numbers of rural Native Americans reside on or near Native American reservations and trust lands in the Midwest plains, [the Rocky Mountain region], the Southwest, and Alaska" (Housing Assistance Council (HAC), 2012), with some states, such as Montana, South Dakota, Wyoming, having more than 80 percent of the total Native population living in rural and small-town areas.

It is important, too, to draw attention to the classification of "rural" in relation to Native populations since Native individuals and communities continue to face systemic erasure from mainstream media, statistics, and research (Shotton et al., 2013). The Census Bureau defines urban as having 50,000 or more people in that area, and a rural area as any place with a population under 2,500 (Sierk, 2017).

Based solely on this definition, Native people who live in communities of more than 2,500 people but less than 50,000—which accounts for many towns in New Mexico, Oklahoma, North Dakota, to name a few—are not recognized as "rural," rendering those communities invisible in rural statistics. In other words, how rural gets defined produces understandings of who gets counted as a rural person. This is one clear example of how the idea of rural is a social construct.

Since information about Native populations is often not presented in research projects and data collection, they are referred to as "Asterisk Nation" by the National Congress of American Indians (NCAI Policy Research Center)—meaning that though Native communities are the longest-standing groups of people in this country, they are often merely represented by an asterisk to indicate there is not enough data to understand the successes, barriers, and unique components of these people and communities.

For the purposes of this chapter, the primary implications of the Native asterisk are widespread misunderstandings about "rural" demographics and reduced visibility of Native communities, which have material effects, including, for example, potential reduction in grants and overall funding, and exclusion from conversations about rurality for rural Native America.

In many respects, such current-day attempts at and practices of erasure are a continuation of the systematic attempts at assimilation and (cultural) genocide for the last 500+ years. From the time of European contact forward, colonial powers conducted genocidal campaigns against Native nations, from massacring entire communities to intentionally severing food pathways (e.g., burning of crops).

For example, the Haudenosaunee Confederacy (Iroquois) nicknamed George Washington, the first president of the United States, "Hanödaga:yas," translated as "Town Destroyer" due to his sanctioned policies of destroying Native villages and their food sources (Michelson, 2018). Other mechanisms of oppression included advertising bounties for the scalps of Native individuals and kidnapping Native children and placing them in boarding schools whose goals were to "Kill the Indian, and save the man" (Churchill, 2004).

During and after these genocidal practices, Native populations were driven out of developing settler places and corralled onto reservation lands, which were, over time, increasingly reduced in size. These actions occurred within the context of federal removal policies and the establishment of federally recognized tribal nations (who were "given" specific allotted lands—and often not very desirable land).

In other words, these were deliberate acts sanctioned by the U.S. government. Moreover, these policies and practices are key aspects of what have led to contemporary understandings of rurality and many Native communities and people. For example, the Indian Removal Act of 1830, signed into law by then president Andrew Jackson, whose face now adorns the $20 bill, removed Native communities who resided east of the Mississippi River from their homelands to lands west of the river in order to make room for the influx of European settlers.

The Indian Appropriations Act of 1851 officially created reservations, which were spaces designated to segregate and control Native people located primarily in parts of the country white settlers did not want to live. The Dawes/General Allotment Act of 1887 divided up Native lands into an individual-ownership system and made lands that had been designated as tribal lands to become available for purchase to non-Natives, driving some Natives out of their federally designated land and into more urban places.

These—and other—intentional genocidal and assimilatory practices exercised in the United States had two aims:

1. to literally annihilate Native people through genocidal practices (e.g., massacres, starvation, forced sterilization); and
2. to assimilate those who were not physically erased into Eurocentric, anglophone cultures through assimilatory boarding schools, culturally and linguistically discriminatory laws and policies, and hegemonic social practices (Dunbar-Ortiz, 2014).

As a result of these assimilatory and genocidal goals of settler colonization, Native individuals, communities, and nations today are often invisible within the mainstream societal spheres of education, law, medicine, policy, media, and arts—all of which reify current-day inequalities in educational, social, behavioral, health, and economic outcomes (Native Report, 2014).

Even though they have never ceased to exist and continuously contribute valuable knowledges and understandings of the world, Native people have, in many respects, "socially disappeared" in the eyes and minds of many non-Native individuals and communities (e.g., Na'Puti, 2019; Brayboy, 2005). One particularly harmful result of the social erasure of Native people is that non-Native people often assume that they can now claim Native lands, cultures, and identities, since they believe Natives "are no longer here."

This historically constructed and contemporary belief is currently maintained through practices of non-Native people wearing Native cultures as costumes or fashion (Friedman, 2019); sports teams appropriating Native identities as mascots (HolyWhiteMountain, 2016); and non-Native people claiming relationships of "indigeneity" or "Native" status to the settler state, city, or property they hail from (e.g., Pearson, 2013; Scott, 2010). The mainstream beliefs that Native people do not exist in rural spaces (or at all) is based on the assumed completion of genocide (Smith, 2016).

Despite these centuries-long attempts of physical and cultural genocide, Native communities' presence and "survivance," which brings together survival and resistance (Vizenor, 2008), can been seen today across many domains in relation to rurality, including law, education, arts, medicine, food, health, and sociopolitical activism. In this way, it is important to note that the intersections of Native issues and rurality is not something from the past but is an important aspect of *contemporary* rural issues and notions of rurality.

For example, in the well-known Dakota Access Pipeline movement (#NoDAPL) in 2016, thousands of Native individuals and hundreds of unique tribal nations, along with non-Native allies, gathered in rural North Dakota in peaceful solidarity to protect the Standing Rock Lakota's sacred water source and ancestral homelands.

In a lesser-known instance that highlights the intersection of modern indigeneity and rural lands, the court case *Herrera v. Wyoming* (2019) reveals how the Apsáalooke (Crow) nation fought for its right "to hunt upon [the land] as long as the game lasts" (p. 402). Specifically, a member of the tribe hunted in a territory during a time of year the Wyoming government does not normally allow, and the tribe brought the case to the Supreme Court, which ruled in their favor, upholding an 1868 Treaty.

Both *Herrera v. Wyoming* and the #NoDAPL movement are powerful examples of contemporary Native people and communities practicing activism, culture, and life in and for rural spaces and exercising their inherent land rights as a present-day sovereign Native nation interacting with the United States government. In these ways, it is imperative that as English educators consider pedagogies within rural contexts and/or related to rurality and "place," the past and present experiences and perspectives of Native communities permeate their thinking and conceptualization of curriculum.

THE INTERSECTIONS OF RURALITY AND AFRICAN AMERICAN COMMUNITIES

Black leadership in sustainable agriculture and food justice movements provides tools for aspiring African-heritage growers to start agricultural projects and heal from the trauma associated with slavery and land-based economic exploitation.

—Soul Fire Farm, 2018, "Farming While Black, in Sunshine and Solidarity"

Invisibility can be used as a tool of oppression, because if people can't be seen, then their work can be discounted, their experience of violence and oppression can go without recourse, and their lives can be devalued.

—Alisa Bierria, Mayaba Liebenthal, and INCITE! Women of Color Against Violence, 2007, "To Render Ourselves Visible: Women of Color Organizing and Hurricane Katrina"

Eight percent of the overall rural population is African American, with "nearly 9 out of 10 rural and small-town African Americans located in the Southern region of the United States" (HAC, 2012, p. 2). Furthermore, "Rural African Americans comprise an even larger portion of the population in the so-called southern 'Black Belt' communities of Alabama, Georgia, Mississippi, North Carolina, South Carolina, and Virginia, as well as the Lower Mississippi Delta states of Arkansas, Mississippi, and Louisiana" (HAC, 2012, p. 2).

The recognition that African American authors, lawyers, teachers, farmers, ideas, knowledge, and contributions exist in rural places generates a more accurate representation of rurality "for if in the American imaginary black people exist only in urban spaces, then the reality of blacks who live in other places is rarely represented or imagined, or considered as real" (Lawrence, 2015, p. 222).

Thus, it is important to recognize how the invisibility of African American populations in rural spaces within the mainstream American imagination was created and how it is maintained.

Normative white perception and understanding of African American identity is inextricably linked to hundreds of years of enslaving practices and white supremacist policies followed by decades-long systemic racism introduced and upheld through economic, political, social, and geographic means.

The cause of invisibility for African Americans in rural communities begins to emerge when these communities are considered within the historical context of how capitalism was/is tied to the enslavement and commodification of people (Smith, 2016); contemporary Jim Crow legacies; current realities of everyday racial microaggressions (Sue et al., 2007); disproportionate and elevated police brutality for African American individuals, and the overrepresentation of African Americans in criminal justice systems (Alexander, 2010).

In 1870—as a result of enslavement and then economic and labor ties—over 80 percent of African Americans lived in the rural south. By 1940, that percentage had decreased to 50 percent, and by 1960, "only 25 percent of the black population was still residing in the rural South" (Price et al., 1970, pp. 47–48). This massive decrease was due in part to the "Great Migration" to urban spaces in the north, as African American populations fled to escape economic limitations, Jim Crow restrictions, and to locate new and different opportunities.

Another contributing factor to the influx of African American populations in northern cities during this time was also due to what sociologist James Loewen dubs the "Great Retreat" (Loewen, 2005). The Great Retreat was the dramatic *decrease* in African American populations in small towns and rural areas across northern states. This shift was a result of "sundown towns," which worked to expel African Americans (and other racially minoritized groups) from rural and suburban communities.

A sundown town, also known as a sunset or a gray town, is a town or city that had ordinances in place barring African Americans from living in the town or being in the town after a certain time of day. This was often enforced through harassment alongside town signs reading, "Whites Only Within City Limits After Dark," among other, more derogatory signage that effectively prohibited African American, Chinese, Jewish, and other marginalized populations from taking up residence in towns that were aiming for all-white populations. According to Loewen, sundown towns were pervasive outside the traditional South, ranging from tiny towns of 500 in Illinois and the Dakotas, to cities of more than 100,000 in Michigan and Ohio (Loewen, 2005).

As Loewen argues, "Driving African Americans out and keeping them out became the 'proper' civic-minded thing to do, in the thinking of many whites of all social strata between about 1890 and 1940, lasting until at least 1968" (Loewen, 2005, p. 49). For example, in 1890, every county in the state of Montana has records of African American residents, and after 1890 counties began seeing a decline in African American residents; now Montana's total African American population is less than 1 percent (Census Bureau, 2018).

Simultaneously, African Americans from the South were moving to cities for economic opportunities and to escape persecution in the South, and

African Americans already living in the North or arriving from the South were being driven out of small-town areas as a result of sundown town practices, which contributed to a massive increase in African American urbanization and a sharp decrease in African American residency in rural communities.

Though the history of African Americans and rurality is quite multifaceted, these are some of the mechanisms whereby the associations between rurality and African American people have become disentangled. As scholar David Todd Lawrence explains, "At the turn of the twentieth century, black space was understood and represented largely as rural, agricultural, and southern. By the mid-1970s, associations with black space had shifted toward the population centers of the urban industrial North" (Lawrence, 2015, p. 222).

In addition to providing historical context, Lawrence explains a case study (2015) of an African American community in rural Missouri that demonstrates how current-day invisibility of African American communities in rural contexts has detrimental material consequences for these communities. Specifically, his study explains particular consequences of urban-normativity and racialized space through the dangerous reality of a rural black community in Pinhook, Missouri.

Pinhook was unacknowledged as a town with residents as the U.S. Army Corps and the Mississippi River Commission made the decision to open the Birds Point-New Madrid Floodway and submerge Pinhook under twenty feet of Mississippi River, without any notice to Pinhook residents. As Lawrence points out, "The fate of Pinhook demonstrates the potentially disastrous consequences of the invisibility of rural blackness for those who live in the spaces it renders unseen" (p. 225).

Thus, he reveals how "space" only becomes a "place" once it has been defined by humans for use and value has been bestowed upon it—places have meaning attached to them and that determines the ways in which those places are valued (or not). Moreover, this study demonstrates an instance wherein an African American community in rural Missouri is not considered a "place," in policy-making decisions, therefore rendering all the people in the community "nonexistent."

The current invisibility of rural African Americans can be attributed to the ideological frameworks that underpin enslavement, segregation, and contemporary institutional racism. These bring to bear doubly dangerous effects on rural African American communities. Specifically, if rurality is an issue of social justice and representative equity, and if even white rural communities are invisible, "when this condition is combined intersectionally with race, especially blackness, the effect is even more destructive, as black bodies in rural areas quickly lose not only their legitimacy to occupy space, but also their legibility as human bodies" (Lawrence, 2015, p. 232).

The consistent ignorance about and disregard for African American populations that comprise the rural landscape precisely illuminates why a movement like Black Lives Matter exists and continues to be powerfully necessary in valuing African American people and the (rural) places they live.

For instance, there is a current trend of weddings taking place on plantation properties in the rural south—an act that upholds a romanticization of slavery and commodifies sites of human degradation (Williams, 2019). Also, we need to look no further than how commonly taught books in secondary English (i.e., *To Kill a Mockingbird*) uphold ideological violence toward African Americans in rural places.

At the same time as these racist practices continue in/about rurality, countless current cultural practices that work *against* racism are located in the rural places where African American communities reside. For example, Leah Penniman's new book *Farming While Black: Soul Fire Farm's Practical Guide to Liberation on the Land,* discusses, among a number of topics, "uplifting the legacy of African diasporic knowledge and farming technologies while acknowledging the fact that our food system is built on stolen land and stolen labor is necessary for developing ways to reform this system and reframe narratives around it" (Soul Fire Farm, 2018). This text provides a striking look into the lives, histories, and futures of Black farmers and represents a neglected perspective in agrarian and rural discourses.

Another example can be found at Pearl and Metra Fryar's home in rural Bishopville, South Carolina. Upon moving into their home in this predominantly white small town, they were told that the community believed "black people don't keep their yards looking nice" (Finney, 2014, p. 127). As a way to embrace his relationship to the outdoors while demonstrating his artistry and countering the racist assumption, Pearl transformed their three-and-a-half-acre lot into a work of topiary art. Today thousands of visitors come from all over the world to see how the trees and shrubs Pearl has rescued from a neighboring nursey are shaped into his landscaped vision of plants, lights, and life. Horticultural groups eagerly learn from Pearl's expertise as he invites people into his yard to show what it means to him to engage the outdoors in his rural town (Finney, 2014).

In another example, BAM Fest, a festival that takes place on the Sunflower River in the Mississippi Delta in the small town of Clarksdale, Mississippi, celebrates this rural area as the Birthplace of American Music, crediting Robert Johnson, the King of the Delta Blues (and arguably the very first rockstar). The organizers and musicians creating this festival center a genre of music created by rural African American artists that is now consumed, built-upon, and enjoyed by people all over the world.

Each of these examples—*Farming while Black,* Pearl's yard, and BAM Fest—demonstrate that while the United States's racialized systems of economics, law, education, and housing have murdered, incarcerated, and rendered invisible (rural) African American individuals and communities, these communities never ceased. In fact, they continue to create economy, culture, arts, and contributions in relationship to the rural landscapes where they reside.

THE INTERSECTIONS OF RURALITY AND LATINX COMMUNITIES

> Gardens and farms are spaces where Latinos who come from rural parts of their countries feel that they are not so far from the lands where they grew up, as they reconstruct natural environments with different varieties of fruits, vegetables, and herbs.
>
> —Thompson, 2011, "Somos del campo": Latino and Latina Gardeners and Farmers in Two Rural Communities of Iowa

> Es algo que me gusta mucho, Diego. Es algo que no quisiera perderlo yo. Es como una tradición o como un pasatiempo. Porque nosotros traemos el monte y el campo en la sangre, yo creo, uno no lo puede dejar.
>
> It is something that I really like, Diego. It is something that I do not want to lose. It is like a tradition or like a hobby. Because we have the forest and the countryside in our blood, I think, I cannot get along without it.
>
> —Ricardo (participant from the article cited above)

Latinx (immigrant) communities make up the largest share of racially minoritized groups in rural America (9 percent of the total rural population), are the fastest-growing ethnoracial minority population in rural America as well as in the country as a whole, and are being recognized as a phenomenon called the New Latino Diaspora (HAC, 2012; Sierk, 2017). With "more than half of all rural and small town Hispanics concentrated in the four states of Texas, California, New Mexico, and Arizona, and just under one-quarter of all rural and small town Hispanics living in Texas alone," it is undeniable that the landscape of rural America consists of Latinx-influenced languages, foods, cultures, and people (HAC, 2012, p. 2).

Furthermore, between the last Census-records (2000–2010), the Hispanic population increased 43 percent, and the Hispanic population growth accounted for more than half of the 27.3 million increase in the total U.S. population, with rural and small-town areas reflecting that larger increase (Humes et al., 2011).

While it is clear that Latinx immigrant communities are not only growing but also increasingly integral to rural places, understanding why these individuals and communities contend with social attack and erasure in dominant discourses about rurality is important. This is often best understood in relation to Latinx immigrants being targeted as linguistically deviant, inherently "criminal," and legally "nonexistent."

Language is one of the entry points for the perception of threat Latinx immigrant communities pose in the social imagination of the United States. In a country that has a long history of linguistic oppression for speakers whose first language is not English (e.g., Davis & Moore, 2014), Spanish language and associated dialects and accents continue to be marginalized and associated with a perception of foreignness, which contributes to a perceived threat to the larger anglophone identity of the United States.

The powerful construction of "the other" (Said, 1978) employed through the concept of linguistic deviance serves to mark these communities as inferior and as posing a threat to the majority population, thus imagining them as permanent foreign threats to the settler colonial state (Smith, 2016), regardless of how long they have been part of it. Additionally, any influx of Latinx immigrants, particularly from Mexico, is often portrayed by mainstream media as being associated with an increase in crime. For example, "the current governor of Arizona has used high crime rates (e.g., from drug cartels along the border) as a rallying cry to gain popular support for tough new anti-immigrant legislation" (O'Leary & Romero, 2011).

The irony of these representations is that *studies in rural areas show that crime rates are actually lower in towns with new, elevated Latinx immigrant populations* (Lichter, 2012). This level of attack on Latinx immigrants has been most prominently displayed in recent years with "Build the Wall" rhetoric and similar othering language.

Furthermore, when Latinx immigrant communities are not being actively attacked for being present in the (rural) United States, they are completely forgotten, which is due, in large part, to the problem that some rural Latinx individuals are undocumented (Farmer & Moon, 2011). Because they are not legally U.S. citizens, they cannot vote and often cannot participate in state and city level government, education, and law, which causes them to remain outside these visible community spaces.

As a result, they are part of and contribute to rural community life that remains largely unseen by non-Latinx residents (Lichter, 2012). Perhaps one way of making sense of this is that while "Latinx people make up about 83 percent of field laborers in the United States, they own only about 3 percent of the farms" (Danish, 2019).

Despite the discriminatory labels and social invisibility Latinx populations encounter in rural places, these (immigrant) communities consistently revitalize "dying" rural small towns, preventing them from becoming "ghost towns," and infuse towns with Latinx-influenced restaurants, cultural events, and entrepreneurial endeavors (e.g., Sulberger, 2011). Furthermore, Latinx populations contribute to economic growth as well since "rural counties with higher proportions of Latinos tend to have lower unemployment rates and higher average per capita incomes" (Hanson, 2016).

While rural Latinx communities often remain underrepresented in discourses of mainstream rural America, they, similar to Native American and African American rural communities, are often thriving places. For example, as a way to showcase everyday Latinx ruralities, Kenyon College professor Clara Román-Odio began the Latinos in Rural America (LiRA) project which explores Latinx lives and experiences in Knox County in rural Ohio.

The project's traveling bilingual exhibit showcases Latinx community members' perspectives about place/displacement, intercultural identities, (in)visibility, aspirations, and cultural heritage, among other topics. Additionally, "the oral history project is rooted in interviews and interactions with members of the community who represent diverse economic conditions, stages of life, and aspirations within the broad social fabric of Knox County" (LiRA Project).

Additionally, in a 2017 study, Jessica Sierk describes how students in a New Latino Diaspora (NLD) community distanced themselves from common understandings of rural. The students share about their experiences attending a majority Latinx high school in a rural community and having classmates from Mexico, Los Angeles, and Guatemala, while simultaneously describing what it's like to be from a rural town. Students explained the distancing between common notions of rurality and their own lived rural experiences by "alluding to an alternative youth subculture influenced by incoming Latino students from cities in Mexico, Guatemala, and California, which they contrasted with the more stereotypical subcultures they observed in neighboring, rural, majority-white communities" (Sierk, 2017, p. 342).

This study contrasts traditional conceptions of rurality with the idea that rural is cosmopolitan and provides a model to begin understanding a different type of rurality (Sierk, 2017). Through these examples, we see how Latinx communities are integral to contemporary notions of rural in the United States.

IMPLICATIONS FOR A CRITICAL RURAL ENGLISH PEDAGOGY

Even though 78 percent of rural America is white (HAC, 2012), using the term "rural" as a code for white is demeaning and inaccurate, as it ignores all other rural residents. Related, it is a mechanism to uphold discourses of white supremacy. As this chapter has illustrated, rural communities have complex, racial histories and present-day challenges and successes, whether or not people "see color" when in a particular rural space. Moreover, rural is not monolithic or simplistic; rather, the people living in rural places promote *ruralities* that require people to engage in and discover communities, place by place.

Thus, as teachers enter and engage in rural schools and communities, it is important to learn the place both as it is and as it was. In so doing, it is important to acknowledge and honor the unique contributions being created and disbursed across people, whether they be by Native, African American, Latinx, white, etc. And then, it is imperative to reconstruct a more representative image of what rural and rurality look and sound like in normative discourse, how it is approached in research, and how (English) educators might best develop pedagogical practices toward these aims.

NOTE

1. For the purposes of this chapter, we use "Latinx" as a collective, inclusive descriptive category for rural residents who identify as having familial, cultural, linguistic heritage connected to countries in Latin America. In instances where other research is cited, their use of "Hispanic" is maintained.

Chapter 6

Opportunities and Challenges in Moving Toward a Critical Rural English Pedagogy

Robert Petrone and Allison Wynhoff Olsen

A Critical Rural English Pedagogy marks rurality as a visible social construct and interrogates it with and through English curricula. In looking across the classrooms of the focal teachers in this book, we can see how at the core of a Critical Rural English Pedagogy is the premise that rurality itself becomes a central area of inquiry within curricula that connects to myriad other issues and topics, as well as English Language Arts standards.

Though uniquely developed and implemented, each of the focal teachers' curricula shares a set of commitments to engaging students at the intersections of rurality, ideology, and power, as well as issues of representation, access, and activism. For Alli, this is done through analysis of literary and media texts to locate how the idea of rural is socially and discursively constructed; for Melissa, this is done by indigenizing place-focused perspectives to interrupt settler colonial renderings and produce more nuanced notions of rural; for Liz, this is done through textual production and distribution whereby students simultaneously celebrate and critique their hometown to imagine innovative possibilities of sustaining and revitalizing rural communities; and for Catherine, this is done by analyzing how rural places and communities construct reputations and identities, particularly as they intersect with gender and race.

Chapter 5 layers into these teachers' enactments of Critical Rural English Pedagogy a much-needed consideration of how issues of race/ism are bound up in rural education and may engender new possibilities for CREP. By exploring some of the historical and contemporary realities of rural communities of color—and by providing some ways of making sense of how and why rurality exists in American consciousness as white—chapter 5 unsettles dominant renderings of rural. In doing so, our hope is that chapter 5 may help rural English teachers imagine pedagogical possibilities that take into consideration how race/ism and rurality intersect.

Taken together, chapters 2 through 5 inspire multiple possibilities for developing pedagogical practices designed to facilitate critical analyses of rurality as a concept and activism to mitigate the marginalization of rural people and communities. Whereas many approaches in rural English Education (as well as place-conscious pedagogies) emphasize making connections between school and community or drawing upon rural as a way to access students' funds of knowledge, CREP asks teachers and students to use their connections both to interrogate the place they call home *and* examine broader notions of rurality.

We recognize that a Critical Rural English Pedagogy requires a deep commitment on the part of English teachers, and how fully a teacher takes on a CREP orientation is as distinct as each teacher, especially since each is located in a particular rural community, in a particular time and space. We also recognize that while notions of context are important for all teachers in any school to consider as they develop pedagogical practices, context has heightened significance for teachers in rural communities given how intertwined communities and schools are in rural places.

Drawing upon our research with rural English teachers, as well as Allison's personal experiences teaching in rural Minnesota, we articulate these connected aspects of rural teaching and place as *community curricular infusions* (Wynhoff Olsen, 2017). By community curricular infusions, we note the continual presence of community in the work of rural teachers and rural education in general. Rural English teaching is so replete with intersections of community that context and curricula cannot be teased apart, and, in many respects, it is counterproductive to try. When rural teachers attempt to sort out what is community and what is school (or curriculum), the divide is felt in the classroom and in teachers' stances toward (and in relationships with) community members. It is a separation that almost ensures teachers remain (or become) outsiders to the community and interrupts the work they aim to achieve with their students.

As such, it is not generative for rural English teachers to develop curricula that focuses solely on disciplinary content knowledge and/or the students in their classes; rather, the community values, land, and sociopolitical ideologies are always already present and coexist as a part of the teaching and learning: they are *infused*. In this way, community curricular infusions speak to the ways that community, curricula, place, values, and teacher positioning and status (within the community) coexist as a part of the teaching and learning in rural English classrooms.

When living rural, community values, land, and sociopolitical ideologies are present alongside and with people's relationships with one another and their connections (or lack thereof) to their place. Thus, when teaching in a rural school, the presence of the community can be considered as both an additional participant and a part of every student and teacher. Rural communities are so infused in teaching experiences that they cannot be set aside as mere contextual consideration. In short, the community is *infused* within the teaching and learning and embodies classrooms viscerally: these community curricular infusions become a part of how teachers do English in rural schools.

Given how integral local context is to rural English teaching, while we encourage rural English teachers to take on a Critical Rural English Pedagogical orientation, we cannot suggest *how* to enact CREP; in fact, as rural itself is not an essentialized entity, neither is CREP. Rather, as the four focal teachers in this book illustrate, each iteration of CREP will be unique and responsive to the local context. In this way, it can be useful to think of a Critical Rural English Pedagogy not as a singular approach but rather as a set of pedagog*ies* that cohere around the central aim of examining, particularly as they pertain to rurality, inequitable power dynamics, ideologies, issues of representation, and possibilities for social activism.

For the focal teachers, each had to immerse herself in her place to learn the values, experience the affordances, hear the silences, and notice the constraints before and/or as she implemented a Critical Rural English Pedagogy. Moreover, questions such as the following can help in this process: How attached am I to this place? Is this place home or am I inhabiting it for a short time? Depending on the answer, teachers make decisions on how to enact CREP and which issues to take up and merge into their curriculu (or not).

By way of recognizing the hard work of taking on and enacting a CREP, the remainder of this chapter considers some of the potential obstacles—as well as opportunities—inherent in many rural communities to manifesting a CREP. To do this, the chapter moves away from individual classrooms and the four focal teachers and includes the full data corpus from the research that first inspired this book (as discussed in the Preface and Introduction). This chapter also takes into consideration subsequent conversations and interactions with rural teachers from around the United States. In this way, we draw upon a wide range of rural English teachers to help illuminate both the challenges and the possibilities for developing and implementing Critical Rural English Pedagogies.

POTENTIAL OBSTACLES IN ENACTING CRITICAL RURAL ENGLISH PEDAGOGIES

The concept of a Critical Rural English Pedagogy proposes radical shifts to how teachers create and offer English curriculum in rural schools. As evidenced by the teachers' experiences highlighted in this book, developing and implementing a Critical Rural English Pedagogy, like much critical work, can be challenging. Alongside the emancipatory possibilities of CREP, challenging students' and community members' perspectives, particularly of their own local context, can often engender push back, "resistance," and even some transgressive behaviors (e.g., racism and shunning those who speak out).

We also recognize that for many rural English teachers, this work may fall into wide-ranging categories from "inspiring" to "work I would love to but simply cannot see myself doing in my classroom." In fact, as we continue to share CREP with rural teachers across the United States, we hear a gamut of responses. Some teachers explain how they feel disconnected from the broader field of English Education and its push to be critically conscious because they experience their communities as "conservative," "monolingual," or "entrenched" in traditional ways of doing English that maintain expectations for standard English from a white, colonial perspective (e.g., canonical literary studies with literary analysis essays with little to no current young adult fiction or examinations of today's sociopolitical climate or use of critical lenses).

Moreover, many of the English teachers with whom we have talked express they often feel alone or among a very small number of people who are trying to push the envelope, so to speak, and often fear pushback from parents, administration, community members, and even students themselves. In other words, they sometimes feel like outliers in their schools and communities. In fact, one teacher recently shared that though she liked her job, she felt she was not able to really build and teach curriculum that aligns with her values and beliefs as an educator because of the broader conservative norms of the community. In this way, her experiences with her own community curricular infusions got in the way of her doing the work she desired to do with her students.

To be clear, leaning into and acknowledging community curricular infusions does not mean that teachers must align themselves to the community's values and perspectives; rather, leaning into and considering their work as part of the infusions indicates their willingness to identify as a rural English teacher in relationship with their particular community: at the level of classroom, school, and surrounding town. In so doing, teachers may yearn for the opportunity to be in relationship with their students and communities in more robust ways, more critical ways, and yet, they do not always feel like this is available. This unavailability may be due to their concerns that if they push too hard, they may have complications in their professional and/or personal lives—things such as not having their contract renewed or being confronted by parents or community members about their curriculum as they head out for a meal at the local café or bar.

Attention from community members, parents, administration, and/or school board members will play out differently for each teacher, as evidenced by the teachers' experiences highlighted in this book. Each of the four focal teachers knew their curriculum was on display in one way or another and that they needed to be prepared to articulate their pedagogical reasoning in the event they were challenged. For example, Melissa had parents walk into her classroom while she was teaching, asking why she was teaching all these "weird" books and talking about whiteness in her classes. Catherine had a parent question her morals and was curious why she was talking about sex with her seniors. Both of these teachers engaged in dialogue with these concerned parents and also spoke with their administrators and colleagues—to which they received mixed responses.

In the four teacher cases in this book, and in others discussed in interviews, teachers mentioned colleagues who supported them but were curious at their willingness to engage in risky curricula. These colleagues (all outside of the English department) wondered why the teachers wanted to draw attention to their work and take up issues that are historically not discussed in rural schools.

To this question we take a moment to respond: Why wouldn't English teachers want to engage their students in critical conversations, particularly in and through the English curriculum—a subject that affords itself to examine the human condition and is rich with diverse authors, perspectives, and modes? We are personally not comfortable telling teachers that students in their particular rural place are not ready for nor able to engage in curricular practices that their peers in urban and suburban sites are being afforded.

Related, other rural teachers interviewed experienced curricular pushback from parents. Some parents called for a censoring of texts or topics that they found inappropriate for myriad reasons, including religious grounds (i.e., teaching witchcraft through the *Harry Potter* series). Other parents wanted teachers to lower the rigor of the work because they found too much time on English projects unnecessary—and their determinations of "too much" were results of comparing the work with recollections of their own homework from twenty-some years ago, in the same school/town.

While these types of challenges may also occur in suburban and urban contexts, teachers in rural communities tend to be under closer scrutiny given their visibility in the community. Several teachers told stories of how parents and board members approached them about their curricula or students' grades while at the local bar, while buying a few items at the local store, while at church, or while outside walking their dogs. When teachers live in their small rural towns—as most do because of the vast distance in between towns—parents and school board members have easy access to them: one can't hide well in a town of 5,000, let alone one with 500 people.

Thus, acknowledging community curricular infusions may help teachers avoid being positioned as one entering a new space (or returning home) as academic elites who are coming to fix or remedy the ills of rural communities. Rather, they can position themselves working alongside and with, *in relationship*, to others in the community and perhaps, use the visibility to their advantage.

We acknowledge that asking rural teachers to take on CREP orientations is asking them to be more visible, more of a target, and often, more separated from their colleagues in their willingness to critique and challenge rural realities (ruralities). In other words, we ask: What are the costs for a teacher being *the* person in a community offering critical issues and critiques in the classroom?

We recognize that teachers' rural contexts create challenges when considering how to add criticality to an already present and overwhelming job. We also know that adding a critical examination to one's (or one's students') home or primary discourse (Gee, 1989) is laden with emotion and potentially fraught with challenges. In addition, English teachers are often the sole English teacher in the school or one of a small number of English teachers—and as such, the curricular pushback may feel like a personal attack.

The emotional toll and exhaustion of accepting work that is often filled with tensions requires patience and endurance that teachers may have in short supply as a result of "teaching thin" (teaching the full department, grades 7–12) and "wearing many hats," as mentioned in the Preface and Introduction. Based on our research with rural English teachers, these contextual features of rural English teachers' jobs most definitely factored into their choices about the extent to which they were able and willing to enact a CREP. What we also learned from our four focal teachers was that their own alliances to their place, as well as how long they intended to teach in their particular school, played a key role.

Consequently, we return to those of you who are inspired by CREP yet see challenges on how to integrate this approach into your rural school and community. First, we hear your concerns. We also recognize that you may be distinct from your colleagues and fellow community members, given your critical orientations or willingness to engage your students in CREP; thus, you may be lonely and/or feel that you have to repress your orientations toward a Critical Rural English Pedagogy.

Given these concerns, a prudent first step for many teachers, particularly those early in their careers and/or new to communities, might be to adopt an ethnographic stance toward the school and community as a way to start building toward a CREP. By an ethnographic stance, we mean that teachers might take on a position of inquiry that seeks to understand and locate the various hot-button topics in the community, barriers that might exist to engage in critical work, and resources in the community that might enable critical work.

Another important aspect of this inquiry work is to help locate allies in the community who might be interested in building alliances. In this way, an ethnographic stance might include a teacher informally canvassing students, parents, administrators, community members, and/or school board members to better understand their perspectives, values, and the sociocultural landscape of the community. This may include an understanding, for example, of a community's or region's resources, collegial networks, and academic aims or goals.

By observing and immersing oneself in the community to inquire and understand, teachers will also be doing the important and necessary work of building relationships with and between the community, students, school, and curriculum—all of which will enable community curricular infusions. Ultimately, an ethnographic stance can help build these necessary relationships as well as locate potential entry points for developing and implementing a Critical Rural English Pedagogy. It is important to understand, too, that this work of inquiry and relationship building—and conceptualizing and developing strategic entry points for a CREP within a community—takes time, patience, and oftentimes, courage.

It is also significant to note that English teachers, in all contexts, receive some curricular pushback when they bring in contemporary works or non-canonical literature. For many stakeholders, there is comfort in the traditional, old, and familiar works, and tensions rise as current issues circulate in classrooms. And yet, disciplinary research indicates that it is not best practice for English teachers to just teach canonical works; rather, students need and deserve texts that provide windows and mirrors (Bishop, 1990) and promote relevance to students' lives (Paris, 2012)—not to mention work against recapitulating settler colonial harm (de los Ríos et al., 2019; Tschida et al., 2014).

In short, curricula that take on contemporary issues, conflicts, and social issues can scare people; in our experience, it is often, though, less about the students and more about parents and community members who do not embrace these critical approaches. Thus, as we continue thinking about how and if we work in schools and communities that enable us to do critical work, we need to also consider ways that we can help teach our administrators and communities how our field is moving and why their students deserve to advance with it. In this way, taking on a Critical Rural English Pedagogy sometimes extends beyond the classroom and into more advocacy at community levels.

LEVERAGING UNIQUE FEATURES OF RURALITY TO ENACT A CRITICAL RURAL ENGLISH PEDAGOGY

While we do not proffer any silver bullets to mitigate potential challenges teachers might encounter when implementing a curriculum that challenges students and/or dominating community ideologies, we do have some suggestions for supporting this work. Specifically, we note several unique features of rural that can be leveraged to take up a Critical Rural English Pedagogy: the time teachers and students have together and one's status in the community. Both of these have a particular rural element to them that is generative when considering CREP.

Learning over Time

It is typical for rural teachers to teach students for multiple years. Thus, the construct of curricular time is fluid and serves as a potential benefit, particularly when teaching a Critical Rural English Pedagogy.

In rural schools, teachers and students have more time than is typical to develop relationships with one another and deepen understandings of complex concepts, as well as time to work through some of the challenging affective dimensions of the work. As Allison experienced with her high school students in MN, due to the multiple years together, "We could read one another's body language, respond to shorthand, and use a shared vocabulary. Not having to start over each year also provided us time and confidence, both of which shaped my teaching and our collective learning" (Wynhoff Olsen, 2020, p. 265).

Teaching siblings and cousins, teachers begin to understand how family trees wrap together. Teachers also start to anticipate the needs of neighboring students and their shared schedules on the farm, particularly as this connects to curricular timing and days of school missed for chores. As time passes and teachers' relationships develop, there are fewer jolts to how the rural lives within a particular place merge with the curricular flow. Teachers can lean in and be fuller participants with the community curricular infusions—rather than stunned outsiders.

Rural school schedules also provide time to learn concepts through multiple exposures (Wynhoff Olsen, 2020). While rural English teachers often feel pressured in creating and delivering their students' complete English program 7–12, there is quite a lot of time to (re)expose students and build critical understandings *incrementally*.

Although we only have access to one unit of study from Alli, Melissa, Liz, and Catherine, we know that each teacher relied on cycles of exposure to enhance her work with students. As shown in the focal case studies, teachers can create lessons that introduce an idea and build exposures for students to grapple with critical tasks in small increments; in subsequent years, teachers can add additional elements and move students into deeper realms of understanding for more sustained periods of time.

This incremental exposure cycle pairs well with rising text complexities in upper grade levels and encourages students to add to their knowledge. Multiple exposures also promote a change or alteration in how students perceive the ELA curriculum and their place in it (e.g., Liz's students shifting their relationships with poetry). Leveraging time through multiple exposures affords opportunities for enhanced student learning and shared engagement in critical work. Together, teachers and students can marinate in their ideas, take breaks when emotions overwhelm and cloud thinking, and add intertextual layers to examine in new ways.

Related, time also respects the wobble (Fecho, 2011) or dissonance (Gorski, 2009) that students may experience as their constructs of rural are examined. As Alli's chapter details, students began using the Critical Rural Perspective and used it throughout the year, knowing that they would continue to use this frame into high school. Given a programmatic rather than single-unit approach to developing curriculum, rural English teachers are able to build critical curriculum in formative ways.

Community Status

As previously explored, relationships between community, parents, school, and teachers are often more pronounced in a rural community. Teachers live next door to their students and dine at restaurants or grab a drink in bars owned by their students' parents or their colleagues. When they shop in town, it is common for their student to be working the till and checking them out (as well as noting what they purchase). Community members are the coaches for teachers' kids, and the whole town shows up for football games and choir concerts, seated side by side one another.

While these "porous boundaries" (Cuervo, 2016) result in constant visibility or surveillance of teachers, the relationships built are significant. Because of this aspect of rural living and teaching, rural teachers can leverage their positionality and use their shifting status to engage in critical work in their classrooms.

The focal teachers in this book, as well as our interviews with rural English teachers, suggest that much of how their curriculum is noticed, accepted, and challenged is dependent on the teacher's status in the community—a status influenced by length of time living and/or working in the community, familial (or lack thereof) connections, and involvement and visibility in the day-to-day life of the community. Though, of course, there are many factors contributing to the receptivity of a teacher's curriculum, their status in the community for rural teachers is a crucial, or potentially "make or break" one.

If teachers (like Liz) are trusted, their curricular choices tend to be supported. If they are active, visible members of the community (like Alli), they receive less questions about new text additions and epistemological shifts. If they challenge students' conceptions of race and place during their first year of teaching at the school (like Catherine and Melissa), they may encounter pushback from parents and community members. Thus, when teachers are rooted in the community and have status that marks them positively, their curricular moves are more easily accepted and questioned less; on the other hand, when teachers have a less stable status (by sheer fact of being new or not being active in the community), concerns may open up and potentially even overwhelm the teacher and/or disrupt the enactment of their curriculum.

A teacher's status is also influenced by the reputation and trust built within the classroom. As rural teachers and students spend multiple years together, they foster their relationships with one another, which afford them access to shared histories and ways of knowing, a shared way of being together in school, and a more nuanced understanding of one another's ideologies and familial situations. This, in turn, influences learning and the opportunity to do critical work.

From Alli, Melissa, Liz, and Catherine, as well as other teachers interviewed, we find a useful question for rural teachers to be: How am I building a reputation as one who does a particular kind of work in this place? Another to consider is this: How am I working in relationship with my community in order to build and enact curricular goals?

In a time when the field of English Education is imploring teachers to participate in our sociopolitical climate through practices such as critical literacy (Morrell et al., 2013) and culturally sustaining pedagogies (Paris, 2012), we encourage rural English teachers to actively consider their positionality and consciously develop their status within their schools and communities.

SUPPORTING CRITICAL RURAL ENGLISH TEACHERS

By working with Alli, Melissa, Liz, and Catherine—as well as many other rural English teachers—we understand that teaching English in rural contexts demands a lot, and that taking up a Critical Rural English Pedagogy demands even more. As teachers engage their students in opportunities to examine constructs of rural, produce more nuanced and culturally accurate texts, and distribute their own renderings of how they are experiencing their communities, teachers partake in celebrations and critiques that redefine the curriculum.

Thus, CREP also reshapes the identities of teachers, and so, we ask: How can teachers who take up the work of a Critical Rural English Pedagogy support themselves and be supported so they can define and sustain their work in rural communities?

Self-Care

We were surprised that, in our interviews, when we asked English teachers what suggestion or recommendation they might have for first-year teachers starting in a rural school, many of them, without thinking, said something along the lines of: "Tell them to find a therapist right away!" We were expecting them to address professional resources, yet these responses, we would soon learn, spoke to an intense need these teachers had for not only professional connection but also personal support.

Given these responses, we have come to understand how vital *self-care* is for rural English teachers, particularly those who are enacting a Critical Rural English Pedagogy. Rural schools and communities cannot continue expecting teachers to "wear all hats" because it takes a toll on their mental and physical health as well as their relationships. When the majority of teachers' time is spent teaching, coaching, advising, and simply giving to the school, little time remains for them to foreground relationships in the role of mom, dad, partner, friend, and so on. This toll gets compounded when teachers take up criticality in their curriculum.

From our research, we urge teachers to acknowledge this overload and to slow down, making time to pay attention to mental, emotional, physical, and spiritual needs for health and wellness. Teachers we interviewed expressed the need for the following, among other supports: (a) access to mental health professionals (e.g., therapist, counselor); (b) space (not at the school) for daily exercise (e.g., gym, yoga studio); (c) more ready access to healthy food (both for dining out and at the local grocery store); and, perhaps most importantly, (d) time—time to cook meals, visit with friends, read a book that is not for work, drive to see a movie. Overall, rural English teachers expressed the need for opportunities to detach from work—mentally and physically—to recharge themselves.

Based on our research, we know that opportunities for self-care are often limited in rural communities. Specifically, there is limited access to counselors, physical therapists, and specialized physicians, as well as only a handful of amenities (e.g., restaurants, movie theaters, workout spaces, and museums), if any at all. Towns typically have a local bar, a gas station that doubles as a market, and multiple churches. Some teachers interviewed use online spaces as both an outlet and a solution. For example, one teacher relied on online resources to deepen her yoga practices and eventually, learned how to teach yoga; she has since started offering web-based yoga classes that she records from her home studio—and makes available to anyone with an internet connection.

Teachers in rural schools also get creative with their days off. One veteran teacher works in a school district that provides a set number of days for leave—sick leave or personal days—that teachers are able to use as they see fit. Given the intense school days and weeks this teacher typically works, she and her husband carve out one or two times during the school year to take mini-vacations together. For them, this is their opportunity to connect and remove themselves from the surveillance and pressures of their small town; they deliberately schedule these times outside of typical school vacations because during those "given breaks," the teacher herself takes time to decompress and find moments to catch her breath and/or catch up on grading, be present in town for lunches or coffee dates, and enjoy the surrounding landscape.

Several teachers interviewed leave their rural communities over the summer months, spending their nonteaching time back in their home places, traveling, or attending professional development workshops in disparate locations; for these teachers, removing themselves from the place where they are known as "the English teacher" is necessary.

With regard to self-care, we also want to (re)articulate that as rural teachers care for their students, they are often deeply familiar with their students' lives given to the social and geographic dynamics of rural teaching discussed in the Preface and Introduction. Thus, these rural teachers are likely shouldering social and emotional burdens and may be experiencing secondary trauma (Thieleman & Cacciatore, 2014).

Because mental health services are often not very accessible in rural communities, rural teachers are often strained even further. When communities lack these resources, the need or impetus for students to share their struggles with their teachers is common. And yet, teachers are not counselors and as such, cannot treat their students; rather, they are to refer them. For, rural teachers, the referral system adds a layer of burden when these next resources are many miles away.

Consequently, we suggest that discussions of rural teacher support involve engaging with other sectors and fields, including human development, social work, psychology, and rural sociology to bring more mental health services to rural and remote areas. During the wait, we recognize rural teachers need support. We also remind people in rural communities that they too need to pay attention to referral systems and be in partnership with teachers so the teachers know how students in their communities can access help.

Building and Participating in Professional Networks

In addition to personal self-care, teachers we interviewed and the focal teachers in this book explained how vital their professional networks were for not only their teaching but also their overall well-being. For example, Alli paused her teaching, completed two years of graduate work, and then returned to her rural district to enact many of the ideas she had developed. Melissa read voraciously and participated in several professional conferences during her first year of teaching. She printed articles and stacked the scholarship on her desk for quick access and reading moments. Liz started grad school while teaching so she could be part of a disciplinary community while teaching. Catherine participated in an online study group that Allison facilitated for early career, rural English teachers, and she also presented at the National Council Teachers of English conference on a rural panel.

All four of these teachers dove into scholarship to support not only the development of their ideas but the justification for it. In their own ways, they built a professional support system that was not afforded to them within their schools or regions. As noted in the Preface and Introduction, teaching is an already isolated profession that gets amplified when teaching in rural school departments of one (or as part of a small English team) in a remote location.

Professionally, most rural English teachers lack opportunity to develop their pedagogy with disciplinary mentors—or even just other English colleagues. There is no hallway chatter to debrief a lesson gone wrong (or right), suggest a new approach to writing instruction, or brainstorm how to lead literary discussions at a given moment in time.

Rural English teachers have a heightened need to adapt disciplinary ideas and practices to their setting because the field of English Education still provides the bulk of curricular and pedagogical foci through the lens of urban and suburban classrooms (Eckert & Alsup, 2015). While all teachers are expected to make modifications and tailor their work to their students, rural teachers lack models in their settings.

What will work well for a class of thirty high school students does not translate into a junior class of seven students who have known each other and been in classes together their entire lives. Thereby, professional development opportunities for rural English teachers are necessary so the teachers can check-in, debrief their practices, and talk with others in similar settings.

Professional networks need more attention and development to the specific needs of rural English teachers, as well as ways of developing and sustaining both an ELA curriculum and program. In a time when teacher retention is low and rural teacher turnover is high, these curricular continuities and visibility have become voids in many rural school districts (Cuervo, 2016).

In our own research, none of the teachers interviewed received a curricular scope and sequence when they were hired; rather, they were given keys to their classrooms and book rooms and received some version of a pat on the shoulder and a "good luck." While many teachers appreciated the freedom to build English programs that suit their preferences rather than having to negotiate with others (or be told what to do), they also felt the pressure of being the only person reviewing the content standards and writing the full curriculum for multiple grade levels.

As it is now many of the districts require teachers to submit lesson plans to their administrator, and yet, no teacher interviewed received any curricular models of what works well in their school sites. Perhaps when a new rural English teacher is hired, administrators or mentor teachers could provide some guidance. As it is now, in single- and/or small-person rural English departments, curricular decisions get attributed to an individual person (aka, whoever the English teacher is at the time) rather than a department or program. This has potential to take an emotional toll, particularly if test scores or standardized outcomes are not aligned with school board, community, and/or parent expectations.

Shouldering the weight of working with all students to mastery is also a burden. As one teacher explained, in a rural school, everyone points to the English department when ACT scores are low, when students dislike reading, or when the community perceives student writing to be subpar. And when the department is you—a department of one or two—that scrutiny feels not only stressful but also like an attack. Furthermore, English, a required subject in all secondary grades, is often positioned squarely as an academic discipline, and English teachers often received pushback and questions of relevancy.

To access professional networks, teachers interviewed have a few key preferences. The first are existing social media platforms. Teachers, particularly those just entering the field, appreciate the online engagement and rely on it to connect with disciplinary colleagues. The teachers also voiced that they invest time in reading teacher blogs because they are curious how other teachers are navigating both curricular choices and the emotional weight of teaching English.

Another often utilized online platform is the currently popular, www.teacherspayteachers.com. This site is one that teachers used to help them avoid building new curricular material for every lesson and class prep, 7–12. Directly related are ways of connecting teachers to broader, professional networks of their choice. We believe that rural English teachers deserve districts monies and time for professional networking in areas of need (e.g., a National Writing Project site to better their teaching of writing).

This district investment might be time carved out for the teacher to travel to the nearest English teacher in the region for regular meetings (to discuss teaching practices in the particular region and school size); it might be money and time to attend and/or present at a professional conference (e.g., The National Council Teachers of English); or it might be money to attend a workshop or class focused on rural English teaching or a particular topic they teach (e.g., Shakespeare) during their summer break. Regardless, it goes a long way for an administrator to hand teachers an invitation and/or a budget to seek out and participate in professional networks and acquire professional resources and community within the discipline.

Rural English teachers also deserve more invitations to connect with English educators who are preparing teachers to enter the field (e.g., Wynhoff Olsen, 2019). Dialogue across teacher educators, in-service teachers, and pre-service teachers promotes the teachers' agency and experiences and affords time for rural English classrooms to be considered in pedagogical and research conversations.

Such collaborations also include field experiences centered in rural communities and schools, as these provide pre-service teachers experiences with rural English teaching in rural schools with rural English teachers; research indicates that these experiences help enact more nuanced understanding of what it means to identify as a rural teacher and affirms that the unique features of rural this book discusses are attractive to incoming teachers (Mitchell et al., 2019). For rural English teachers, these collaborative and layered networks also provide professional mentoring that can help retain teachers once they are in their teaching placements.

Finally, rural teachers deserve more time to interact professionally while "at home" in their schools and districts. We suggest that administrators build academic calendars and workday schedules to provide time for the teachers who are in the district—across disciplines and grade levels—to connect around academics (Wynhoff Olsen & Branch, 2018).

As we traveled to schools it was obvious that the teaching staff in most buildings gathered often around social events—whether it be pot lucks at the teachers' apartment building, trivia night in town, or promoting school spirit. What was less apparent, however, was a set of teachers holding professional conversations. Professional development days were minimal, compared to larger, more suburban districts, and faculty meetings focused on school policies, upcoming events, and/or non-discipline specific topics.

Certainly, a lack of academic planning time for teacher teams is due in part to the single-person departments, but we encourage rural administrators to provide time for teachers to find common ways forward, using their distinct disciplinary knowledge plus the knowledge of the students and place create a more connected curriculum. This might result in team teaching, interdisciplinary activities and units, or simple meetings that focus on students' experiences in school—a common ground rural teachers have.

We recognize that this will not solve the void of disciplinary colleagues, but it will afford teachers time to interact as professionals within their particular rural school. It is also possible that providing time for rural teachers within a district to come together for curricular and academic conversations may spark collaborative, innovative curricular experiences.

Advocacy

Taking on a Critical Rural English Pedagogy does not begin and end within the walls of the classroom. Working toward issues of equity, social justice, and critiquing dominant depictions of rurality necessitates an advocacy by, with, and for rural teachers and allies.

Teachers who take up CREP work to nuance diminished pictures of rurality. They themselves become critical examiners, producers, and distributers of texts. For some teachers, like Alli, Melissa, Liz, and Catherine, this takes the form of writing and presenting, both about their curricular moves and their own ways of situating rural within their classrooms. Melissa also mentioned her activism as she aligned herself with those in the #NODAPL movement, traveling to stand in solidarity and physically engage in taking a stand for land rights.

These opportunities to mitigate the marginality of rural life, rural peoples, rural lands, and rural teaching are becoming increasingly prevalent. The field of English Education is vocal about its expectations that teachers take part in this civic discourse, and we feel that those who enact a Critical Rural English Pedagogy hold similar aims. Building coalitions with other rural teachers and advocates can be one way to engage in this work.

Another way a CREP teacher may advocate is by building coalitions with urban teachers and advocates. Together, rural and urban teachers can dissect texts, produce curriculum, and distribute their ideas within their classrooms and communities; then, as each enacts their curriculum with their students, the work has opportunity to truly flourish. Imagine the dialogue among students and the ways of using web-based video calls, vlogs, and Twitter feeds, all around critiques of both rural and urban spaces.

While such interactions may engender intense emotions and dissonance, CREP teachers can embrace the wobble and use the time afforded to them to unpack, dialogue, articulate, and fine-tune their messages and understandings of what it means to be a particular person at a particular time in a particular space. This kind of teaching and learning is both wholly relevant and humanizing and well within the purview of the English Language Arts.

Beyond these classroom-level collaboratives, rural educators can link with their urban counterparts to build coalitions that work across both contexts to mitigate inequitable systemic issues that affect both rural and urban areas. In this way, a Critical Rural English Pedagogy can help work against rural-urban divides to bring people together to fight for the joint aim of social justice.

Advocacy for rural teachers and schools needs to increase at the level of teacher education. First, universities that provide teacher preparation programs can make rural teaching visible. This might be done through rural field experiences (Mitchell et al., 2019), scholarships for students who student teach in rural communities, and/or course collaborations between pre-service and in-service teachers and rural classrooms (Petrone & Rink, 2020; Wynhoff Olsen, 2019). University programs can also invest their time and shift expertise to examine and reframe courses to more clearly articulate challenges and affordances of teaching in rural schools.

On the state level, offices of public instruction can offer incentives for universities and rural schools to dialogue and collaborate. The varying stakeholders could also offer rural teachers free or reduced tuition graduate programs.

Related, it would also be prudent for universities to develop a certificate in rural education, so professors and students wishing to deepen their knowledge receive recognition for their knowledge. This also stamps approval onto the work in significant and necessary ways. States could also partner with school districts to incentivize rural teachers through signing bonuses, increased salaries, and an invitation to participate in strong insurance and retirement programs.

At the federal level, loan forgiveness programs need to be expanded to be more prevalent and inclusive for rural teachers. Statistics across the country indicate low teacher salaries in general, with higher amounts being paid to suburban and urban teachers (Mitchell, 2018). An examination of university costs set alongside a rural teacher's salary indicates a substantial inequity; teachers struggle to pay back their student loans, pay rent or mortgage, car loans, health insurance, personal fitness, and groceries.

Housing is another key issue for rural teachers. To illustrate, Montana is filled with resort living, national parks, and hunting land, so finding housing is a challenge. Add a low salary to that reality, and teachers struggle to find a place to live in the towns in which they teach. Given the vastness of the state and the regions sparse in incorporated towns as well as nearly nine months of inclement weather, asking a rural teacher to commute long distances daily is neither practical nor is it safe or prudent. Some rural school districts market a hiring package centered around teacher housing: an enticement that is still scarce enough in Montana that those districts who have it are able to use to attract candidates.

A handful of the teachers interviewed lived in apartment complexes, trailer homes, or houses owned by their school district. Each explained how their living situation was necessary, given the lack of options in town. A few shared that the low rent encouraged them to build a financial plan to attack student loans or build up a savings account while teaching for the district; interestingly, these teachers planned to begin their careers in their current rural school and move on to another district later, when they hoped to have a more solid financial grounding.

Other teachers interviewed who own their homes explained that if hired now (and in the last five to ten years), they would never be able to afford to do so on a teacher's salary. And still, other teachers were frustrated that their salaries were low and thus, kept them from purchasing homes; for them, taking a nonteaching job that paid more, in a larger city, was more enticing than the "gift" of teacher housing.

CONCLUSION

In many respects, the conclusion of this book is a beginning—an invitation to continue the work begun here, which, of course, builds upon critical work already being done elsewhere in the field of English Education. Our hope is that the work of the teachers highlighted throughout this book's pages, as well as the perspectives offered on issues of social justice, equity, and intersectionality in chapters 1 and 5, will help advance thinking, research, and teaching in rural schools. We also hope that through this book, more rural teachers can see themselves and their classrooms as sites of critical engagement.

Throughout our research we met with rural English teachers who want to be heard; their rural voices are not yet a cacophony of experience foregrounded in the field, and this book, in many ways, is an attempt toward changing that. We recognize that moving toward a CREP is not easy, but we believe that it holds the promise to engender a more equitable society, particularly related to rural communities and people.

Appendix A
Assignment Sheet for Textbook Entry Project

TEXTBOOK ENTRY RESEARCH PROJECT:
TRIBAL NATIONS OF TODAY (80 POINTS)

Purpose: The purpose of this assignment is to acknowledge (particularly in schools!) that there are gaps in learning and understanding about Native Peoples, histories, cultures, and events.

With what you have been learning and discussing in class through the novel, *Wind from an Enemy Sky*, information about #NoDAPL, lectures, and additional texts, you are becoming well-informed on these topics, with more knowledge, information, and accuracy than what is available in most currently used history textbooks. Thus, we are going to create updated versions of a classroom textbook.

Role: You are a writer for a textbook

Audience: Ninth to tenth grade students

Format: Coupled with your own research, you will draw on the topics you've learned about in the #NoDAPL movement and that have been presented in the novel *Wind from an Enemy Sky* to write an entry for a high school history textbook about a topic of your choice.

Topic: You will select a research topic that relates to the historical or cultural depictions in the novel. (See options below.)

REQUIREMENT CHECKLIST

- 750–1,000 words (5 pts.)
- Written in third person (as most textbooks are) (5 pts.)
- Formatted as a history textbook entry (10 pts.)

- This means you should format your actual document to look like an entry in the textbooks we've analyzed
- Must find and utilize at least **2** outside sources (these must be cited in a separate document) (10 pts.)
  - **The reliability of your outside research sources is of utmost importance (since this is a textbook entry that your peers and others will be reading!)**

  Do NOT use Wikipedia.

- Must include at least **1** image to support your textbook entry (10 pts.)
  a. Images *must* be historically or currently accurate and depict your topic and Native Peoples specifically (e.g., no random horses and/or feathers and/or war-paint)
- Please include, in a separate document, at least **5** quotes/pieces of textual evidence from the novel, *Wind from an Enemy Sky*, that support your topic/research. (10 pts.)
  a. With each piece of textual evidence, please include a three- to five-sentence summary of how that quote helped facilitate your thinking about your textbook/research topic.
  b. Include page numbers with your textual evidence.
- Holistic content, accuracy, interpretation, and quality of textbook entry (30 pts.)

TOPICS

- **Current Indigenous movement that is related in some way to this novel**
  - An example of this is the #NoDAPL movement—how does this situation compare to the dam in this book (which is also the actual dam on the Flathead Reservation in Montana)?
  - Another instance is the oil/gas releases in the Badger Two-Medicine wilderness. How does this compare with the issues of the dam/land in the book?
- **Education**
  - What were the circumstances and effects of the boarding schools? Think about how and why they existed and what impacts they may have on current indigenous populations.
    - All throughout the novel there are instances of boarding school era scenes and Chapter 14 has many that particularly pertain to Antoine's experiences going to, be at, and coming home from boarding school
- **Names/Translation of names**

- How does this topic show up in our society? Think about the translation and consequent changing of names of tribal nations and Native Peoples that was done.
- "He was named Bull—that was the English form of it. But the words men speak never pass from one language to another without some loss of flavor and ultimate meaning" (2).
- Son Child (78), The Boy, and Henry Two-Bit also have instances in the book where their names are translated incorrectly.
- **Water**
  - How can you think about how Native tribes and Peoples are connected to the land and the resources (like water) on/in the land? What do some of these specific relationships with resources look like? How are these relationships understood (or not) by non-Native People and cultures?
    - "They had killed the water" (3). "How can a stream out of the mountains be killed?" (14).
    - "Just the same, you will remember what happened today. After a while you will understand it. The white man makes us forget our holy places. He makes us small" (9).
- **Communication/miscommunication and misunderstanding**
  - Where, how, and why are there instances of (mis)communication between Native Peoples and non-natives? When, where, and how does it seem like non-natives do not understand Native peoples, and why? How is ethnocentrism at play?
    - "The Indian people start from origins about which we speculate but know next to nothing. We do know they are a people who are unlike us—in attitude, in outlook, and in destination" (51).
    - Mid-summer dances: "Naturally, I don't tell them my job is to do away with their 'non productive' dances" (35).
  - Rafferty is wondering about who says the tribe's dances are "non productive" and why—do they have the right to?
    - "Nobody in Washington tells you about medicine bundles" (35).
- **Language**
  - How does speaking different languages play a role between the lens, cultures, beliefs, and understandings of the world between Native Americans and non-natives? What gets "lost in translation," so to speak? Why/how is language and its use important?
    - "He had started to speak in English, as he could do around white men, but he kept slipping back into his own language, then into English, like a man following a vanishing trail" (124).

Appendix B
Student Sample

NATIVE LANGUAGES AND HOW THE MEANING IS LOST DURING TRANSLATION

There are languages all across the world that are interpreted and translated differently, but Native American languages have had a large loss of meaning within the translations. Native nations often had a base for their languages, but at the same time each language was their own. The Apsaalooke and Lakota tribes both have a base of a Siouan language, but both have a unique twist within their languages, which is why one is the Apsaalooke language and the other is Lakota language. In this section, we are going to discuss some of the true meanings and feelings that were lost, and continue to be lost, in the translations of their native languages.

Taking from the Culture

Oftentimes when someone is learning about a culture or religion in a classroom, or just on their own time, they learn about that culture's language. Language of any culture has always held a large meaning to each culture. Language is especially a large part to the Native cultures; it is part of the way their cultures ways of understanding the world are created. When a Native people speak his or her language there is a lot more behind the word than what has been translated. Names and everyday words often are much stronger in meaning then the words we use on a daily basis. Native languages hold many more meanings and feelings behind each word than European interpretations of the language ever contain.

When one language is spoken to someone who may not understand it, but tries to translate, many misunderstandings are made and so meaning is lost.

Native language is a symbol of who specific nations are, and is a representation of their culture and beliefs. It's the story of how they live and breathe. Their language *is* their culture. The Apsaalooke language is different in slight ways compared to the Lakota, even if they share the same language base. They seem similar, but each holds a different meaning or has a slightly different vowel sound. They can use the same letters in writing, but maybe they are used in different ways or describe different things. Languages provide great uniqueness between each tribal nation within the United States. It reveals each nation's different cultures and beliefs.

Misunderstandings

When a language is being translated it is often by someone who understands both languages to some extent. But how is an outsider to the language meant to understand correctly what the meaning is behind a word if that person is not taught by the creators and holders of the language? This is how misunderstandings begin. People try to learn one another's language and properly translate each word to meet their own, but this is not always possible. One word in a Native language could mean multiple words in English. For example, "ahyoka" in Cherokee, means "she brought happiness." But how much of the Cherokee meaning of this word is lost in translating it to those three English words?

Historically, Native Peoples' names and names for tribal nations were often confused or shortened in meaning. When Natives heard their "white" name it often hurt them and felt like they were no longer whom they truly were. Lots of words were misunderstood and are still not corrected today. If one were to speak to a Native person and ask them to speak or translate their Native language while you ask Google as well, likely there will be two different meanings, because Google cannot capture culture like a human can.

Languages are always misinterpreted throughout history by other cultures. A clash that happened between tribal nations and white settlers was at times over the inability to understand one another, and the misinterpreted words and cultures led to arguments and wars. Native nations also often also named other nations based on their own language, which didn't mean that what the tribal nation called themselves.

Lost between Translations

When you are trying express your feelings to someone about something you feel very passionate about, you often do not want them to lose the meaning between the exchanging of your words. This is what happens when one language clashes with another and someone tries to translate the meanings and feelings are left out and thrown away—lost.

We move throughout time and life never truly thinking about all the true meanings behind words that have been misplaced or just lost in all. People's hearts and souls lie in stories and words on a wall or piece of paper that people just throw away and translate for what they see it or want it to be, regardless of the harm that causes. Teachers sometimes teach about Native tribal nations and cultures, but it's often just the "major" tribes. Cultures and languages are grouped all into one and forgotten that there are multiple different ones with different stories. Language is the way people keep their ancestors alive within themselves, so when people just generalize it all and forget the true meanings behind the languages, they are being disrespected without someone's, anyone's, knowing about them and their lives. The things lost in translations are things we need to find and put back where they properly belong. These things are the meanings of cultures that exist behind and inside the words.

Note: The author of this entry is a White student from Park City, Montana. She recognizes that the perspective of language represented in this article is her own non-Native perspective and is influenced by many factors in her own life. She hopes to contribute as an ally to a more accurate view of Native folks in textbooks, but knows the best people to write about Native languages are Native people who speak those languages.

Sources

http://opi.mt.gov/pdf/IndianEd/Resources/MTIndiansHistoryLocation.pdf

http://www.native-languages.org/montana.htm

References

Adichie, C.N. (2009, July). The danger of a single story [Video file]. Retrieved from https://www.ted.com/talks/chimamanda_adichie_the_danger_of_a_single_story/transcript?language=en

Alexander, M. (2010). *The new Jim Crow: Mass incarceration in the age of colorblindness*. New York: The New Press.

Apple, M. (2004). *Ideology and curriculum* (3rd Edition). New York: Routledge.

Appleman, D. (2009). *Critical encounters in high school English: Teaching literary theory to adolescents* (2nd Edition). New York: Teachers College.

Au, W. (2009). Decolonizing the classroom: Lessons in multicultural education. *Rethinking Schools, 23*(2).

Azano, A. (2011). The possibility of place: One teacher's use of place-based instruction for English students in a rural high school. *Journal of Research in Rural Education, 26*(10), 1–12.

Azano, A., & Stewart, T. (2015). Exploring place and practicing justice: Preparing pre-service teachers for success in rural schools. *Journal of Research in Rural Education, 30*(9), 1–12.

Azano, A.P. (2014). "Rural. The other neglected "R": Making space for place in school libraries." *Knowledge Quest, 43*(1), 60–65.

Azano, A.P. (2015). "Addressing the rural context in literacies research." *Journal of Adolescent and Adult Literacy, 59*(3), 267–269.

Battiste, M. (2002). *Indigenous knowledge and pedagogy in first nations education: A literature review with recommendations*. Ottawa: Indian and Northern Affairs Canada.

Bear, C. (Interviewer). (2008, May 12). American Indian boarding schools haunt many. [NPR audio podcast]. Retrieved from https://www.npr.org/templates/story/story.php?storyId=16516865

Behrens, A. (2017). "We're not much to look at": Resisting representations of rurality using a critical rural perspective (unpublished master's thesis). Montana State University, Bozeman, MT.

References

Bierria, A., & Liebenthal, M. (2007). To render ourselves visible: Women of color organizing and hurricane. In South End Press Collective (Ed.), *What lies beneath: Katrina, race, and the state of the nation* (pp. 31–42). Cambridge, MA: South End Press.

Bigcrane, R., & Smith, T. (Directors). (1990). *The place of the falling waters*. [Motion picture documentary]. United States: Salish Kootenai College.

Bishop, R.S. (1990). Mirrors, windows, and sliding glass doors. *Perspectives, 6*(3), 555–565.

Bittle, C., & Azano, A.P. (2016). Constructing and reconstructing the 'rural school problem': A Century of Rural Education Research. *Review of Research in Education, 40*(1), 298–325.

Borsheim-Black, C. (2015). "It's pretty much white": Challenges and opportunities of an antiracist approach to literature instruction in a multilayered white context. *Research in the Teaching of English, 49*(4), 407–429.

Borsheim-Black, C., & Sarigianides, S. T. (2019). *Letting go of literary whiteness: Antiracist literature instruction for white students*. New York: Teachers College Press.

Borsheim-Black, C., Macaluso, M., & Petrone, R. (2014). Critical literature pedagogy: Teaching canonical literature for critical literacy. *Journal of Adolescent & Adult Literacy, 58*(2), 123–133.

Boylan, C., & McSwan, D. (1998). Long-staying rural teachers: Who are they? *Australian Journal of Education, 42*(1), 49–65.

Brayboy, B. (2005). Toward a tribal critical race theory in education. *The Urban Review, 37*(5), 425–446.

Brooke, R.E. (Ed). (2003). *Rural voices: Place-conscious education and the teaching of writing*. New York: Teachers College.

Burton, M., Brown, K., & Johnson, A. (2013). Storylines about rural teachers in the United States: A narrative analysis of the literature. *Journal of Research in Rural Education, 28*(12), 1–18.

Carr, P.J., & Kefalas, M.J. (2009). *Hollowing out the middle: The rural brain drain and what it means for America*. Boston: Beacon Press.

Census Bureau Quick Facts. (2018). Retrieved from https://www.census.gov/quickfacts/MT

Census Viewer. (2012). Retrieved from http://censusviewer.com/city/MT/Park%20City

Chandrashekar, S. (2018). Not a metaphor: Immigrant of color autoethnography as a decolonial move. *Cultural Studies and Critical Methodologies, 18*(1), 72–79.

Cherry-McDaniel, M. (2016). The precarious position of the Black settler pedagogue: Decolonizing (De-weaponizing) our praxis through critical reading of Native feminist texts. *English Journal, 106*(1), 38–44.

Churchill, W. (2004). *Kill the Indian and save the man: The genocidal impact of American Indian residential schools*. San Francisco, CA: City Lights.

Comber, B. (2016). *Literacy, place, and pedagogies of possibility*. New York: Routledge.

Crenshaw, K. (1991). Mapping the margins: Intersectionality, identity politics, and violence against Women of Color. *Stanford Law Review, 43*(6), 1241–1299.

Cuervo, H. (2016). *Understanding social justice in rural education.* New York: Palgrave Macmillan.
Danish, M. (2019, April 15). More Latinx farmers own their land: Could they make the food system more sustainable? *Civil Eats.* Retrieved from https://civileats.com/2019/04/15/ag-census-more-latinx-farmers-own-their-land-could-they-make-the-food-system-more- sustainable/
Davis, T.Y., & Moore, W.L. (2014). Spanish not spoken here: Accounting for the racialization of the Spanish language in the experiences of Mexican migrants in the United States. *Ethnicities, 14*(5), 676.
Delgado, R., & Stefancic, J. (2001). *Critical race theory: An introduction.* New York: NYU Press.
de los Ríos, C.V., Martinez, D.C., Musser, A.D., Canady, A., Camangian, P., & Quijada, P.D. (2019). Upending colonial practices: Toward repairing harm in English education. *Theory into Practice, 58*(4), 359–367.
Diamond, N., Bainbridge, C., & Hayes, J. (Directors), Bainbridge, C., Fon, C., & Ludwick, L. (Producers). (2009). *Reel Injun* [Motion picture documentary]. Canada: Rezolution Pictures.
Donehower, K., Hogg, C., and Schell, E.E. (2007). *Rural literacies.* Carbondale, IL: Southern Illinois.
Drum, K. (2017, April 24). How white is "rural America"? *MotherJones.* Retrieved from https://www.motherjones.com/kevin-drum/2017/04/how-white-rural-america/
Dunbar-Ortiz, R. (2014). *An Indigenous people's history of the United States.* Boston, MA: Beacon Press.
DuVernay, A. (Director) (2016). *13th* [Motion picture documentary]. United States: Kandoo Films.
Dyson, A.H. (2016). *Negotiating a permeable curriculum: On literacy, diversity, and the interplay of children's and teachers' worlds.* New York: Garn Press.
Earling, D.M. (2002). *PermaRed.* New York: Blue Hen Books.
Eckert, L.S., & Alsup, J. (2015). *Literacy teaching and learning in rural communities: Problematizing stereotypes, challenging myths.* New York: Routledge.
Eckert, L.S., & Petrone, R. (2013). Raising issues of rurality in English teacher education. *English Education, 46*(1), 68–81.
Eggers, D. (2006). *What is the what.* San Francisco, CA: McSweeney's.
Eppley, K. (2010). Picturing rural America: An analysis of the representation of contemporary rural America in picture books for children. *Rural Educator, 32*(1), 1–10.
Eppley, K. (2011). Reading mastery as pedagogy of erasure. *Journal of Research in Education, 26*(13), 1–5.
Executive Office of the President. (2014, Dec). Native youth report. Retrieved from https://obamawhitehouse.archives.gov/sites/default/files/docs/20141129nativeyouthreport_final.pdf
Farmer, F.L., & Zola, M.K. (2009). An empirical examination of characteristics of Mexican migrants to metropolitan and nonmetropolitan areas of the United States. *Rural Sociology, 74*(1), 220–40.

Fecho, R. (2011). *Teaching for the students: Habits of heart, mind, and practice in the engaged classroom.* New York: Teachers College Press.

Finney, C. (2014). *Black faces, white spaces: Reimagining the relationship of African Americans to the great outdoors.* Chapel Hill, NC: The University of North Carolina Press.

First Nations Development Institute. (2017). *Research Note: "Twice invisible: Understanding rural native America"* Longmont, CO: First Nations Development Institute.

Friedman, V. (2019, September 13). Dior finally says no to Sauvage: Why luxury fashion and cultural appropriation are on a collision course. *The New York Times.* Retrieved from https://www.nytimes.com/2019/09/13/style/dior-sauvage-cultural-appropriation.html

Fort Laramie Treaty. (1851). Retrieved from https://indianlaw.mt.gov/Portals/127/fortpeck/treaties/laramie%20treaty%201851.pdf

Fort Laramie Treaty. (1868). Retrieved from http://www.pbs.org/weta/thewest/resources/archives/four/ftlaram.htm

Freire, P. (1970). *Pedagogy of the oppressed.* New York: Continuum.

Gee, J.P. (1989). Literacy, discourse, and linguistics: Introduction. *The Journal of Education, 171*(1), 5–176.

Gorski, P. (2010). Cognitive dissonance as a strategy in social justice teaching. *Multicultural Education, 17*(1), 54–57.

Gruenewald, D.A. (2003). Foundations of place: A multidisciplinary framework for place-conscious education. *American Educational Research Journal, 40*(3), 619–654.

Guinier, L. (2004). From racial liberalism to racial literacy: *Brown v. Board of Education* and the interest-divergence dilemma. *The Journal of American History, 91*(1), 92–118.

Hanson, B. (2016, June 24). Immigrants and Latinos bring economic growth to rural communities. *Center for Rural Affairs.* Retrieved from tps://www.cfra.org/news/160624/part-2-immigrants-and-latinos-bring-economic-growth-rural-communities

Hayes, K. (2016, October 28). How to talk about #NoDAPL: A native perspective. *Truthout.* Retrieved from https://truthout.org/articles/how-to-talk-about-nodapl-a-native- perspective/

Heldke, L. (2006). "Farming made her stupid." *Hypatia, 21*(3), 151–165.

Herrera v. Wyoming. (2019). The Supreme Court: Leading cases. *Harvard Law Review, 133*(402), 402–411.

HolyWhiteMountain, S. (2016, October 26). The great failure of the Indians mascot debate? Thinking of it only as racism. *ESPN.* Retrieved from https://www.espn.com/mlb/story/_/id/17891581/great-failure-indians-mascot- debate-thinking-only-racism

Horner, M. (2016, November 7). Sleeping in a tent in North Dakota. In November. But there's more, so much more [blog post]. Retrieved from http://melissamhorner.wixsite.com/mmh1/single-post/2016/11/09/I-Slept-in-a- Tent-in-North-Dakota-In-November-But-Theres-More

Horner, M. (2019). Resistance, reception, race, and rurality: Teaching non-canonical texts in a white conservative, Montana context. In M.V. Blackburn (Ed.), *Adventurous thinking: Students' rights to read and write* (pp. 57–67). Urbana, IL: National Council of Teachers of English.

The Housing Assistance Council (HAC). (2012). *Rural research briefs: "Race and ethnicity in rural America"* Washington, DC: The Housing Assistance Council.

Hudson, M. (2017, February 22). Tempers flare over deleted Cat Country post calling for separate Native tourneys. *Billings Gazette*. Retrieved from https://billingsgazette.com/news/local/tempers-flare-over-deleted-cat-country- post-calling-for-separate/article_c4dd1511-f71c-500c-948e-fe5d0b8e07fb.html

Humes, K.R., Jones, N.A., & Ramirez, R.R. (2011). *Overview of race and Hispanic origin: 2010. 2010 census briefs*. Washington, DC: U.S. Census Bureau.

Johnson, L. L. (2018). Where do we go from here? Toward a Critical Race English Education. *Research in the Teaching of English 53*(2), 102–124.

Kaur, R. (2014). *Milk and honey*. Kansas City, KS: Andrews McMeel Publishing.

Kemmick, E. (2016, August 30). All of Montana is a border town. *Billings Gazette*.

Kirschner, A., Berry, E., & Glasgow, N. (2006). The changing faces of rural America. In Kandell, W., & Brown, D. (Eds.) *Population change and rural society* (pp. 53–74). Netherlands: Springer Publishing.

Latinos in Rural America Project (LiRA). Kenyon College. Retrieved from https://www.kenyon. edu/academics/departments-programs/latinoa-studies/lira/

Lawrence, D.T. (2015). The rural black nowhere: Invisibility, urbannormativity, and the geography of indifference, *The Journal of the Midwest Modern Language Association, 48*(1), 221–244.

Lichter, D.T. (2012). Immigration and the new racial diversity in rural America. *Rural Sociology, 77*(1), 3–35.

Loewen, J. (2005). *Sundown towns: A hidden dimension of American racism*. New York: Touchstone.

Love, B. (2019). *We want to do more than survive: Abolitionist teaching and the pursuit of educational freedom*. Boston: Beacon Press.

Macy, B. (2018). *Dopesick: Dealers, doctors, and the drug company that addicted America*. Boston: Little, Brown and Company.

McCombs, E. (2016, November 30). Girl has perfect response to offensive assignment to "dress like an Indian." *Huffington Post*. Retrieved from https://www.huffpost.com/entry/girl-has-perfect-response-to-offensive-assignment-to-dress-like-an-indian_n_583dcc75e4b0860d6116acc0

McLure, C., & Reeves, C. (2004). *Rural teacher recruitment and retention: Review of the research and practice literature*. Charleston, WV: Appalachia Educational Laboratory.

McNickle, D. (1988). *Wind from an enemy sky*. Albuquerque, NM: University of New Mexico Press.

Michelson, A. (2018). Hanödaga:yas (Town Destroyer) and Mantle. *Third Text, 32*(5–6), 689–692.

References

Miner, H. (1956). Body ritual among the Nacirema. *American Anthropologist, 58*(3), 503–507.

Mitchell, M. (2018, June 18). The effect of teacher shortages on rural areas. The council of state governments. Retrieved from https://knowledgecenter.csg.org/kc/content/effect-teacher-shortages-rural-areas

Mitchell, R., Wynhoff Olsen, A., Hampton, P., Hicks, J., Long, D., & Olsen, K. (2019). Rural exposure: An examination of rural fieldwork opportunities and methodologies in three universities in the U.S. and Australia. *The Rural Educator, 40*(2), 12–22.

Montana Office of Public Instruction. (2019). Essential understandings regarding Montana Indians. Retrieved from https://opi.mt.gov/Portals/182/Page%20Files/Indian%20Education/Indian%20Education%20101/essentialunderstandings.pdf

Montana Office of Public Instruction: Growth and enhancement of Montana students. (n.d.). Retrieved from https://gems.opi.mt.gov

Montana Office of Public Instruction: Indian Education Division. (1999). Constitution of Montana—Article X: Education and public lands. Retrieved from https://opi.mt.gov/ Portals/182/Page%20 Files/Indian%20Education/Indian%20Education%20101/ ArticleX_IEFA.pdf

Montana Office of Public Instruction: Indian Education People, Place, & History. (n.d.). Map of tribal territories in Montana section. Retrieved from http://opi.mt.gov/Educators/Teaching-Learning/Indian-Education/People-Place-History

Morrell, E., Duenas, R., & Garcia, V. (2013). *Critical media pedagogy: Teaching for achievement in city schools*. New York: Teachers College Press.

Na'puti, T.R. (2019). Speaking of indigeneity: Navigating genealogies against erasure and #RhetoricSoWhite. *Quarterly Journal of Speech, 105*(4), 495–501.

NCAI Policy Research Center. The asterisk nation. Retrieved from http://www.ncai.org/ policy-research-center/research-data/data

Nixon, R. (2011). *Slow violence and the environmentalism of the poor*. Cambridge: Harvard.

NYC Stands with Standing Rock Collective. (2016). #StandingRockSyllabus. Retrieved from https://nycstandswithstandingrock.wordpress.com/standingrocksyllabus/.

O'Leary, A.O., & Romero, A.J. (2011). Chicana/o students respond to Arizona's antiethnic studies bill, SB 1108: Civic engagement, ethnic identity, and well-being. *Aztlán: A Journal of Chicano Studies, 36*, 9–36.

Paceley, M.S. (2018). Gender and sexual minority youth in nonmetropolitan communities: Individual- and community-level needs for support. *Families in Society, 97*(2), 77–85.

Paris, D. (2012). Culturally sustaining pedagogy: A needed change in stance, terminology, and practice. *Educational Researcher, 41*(3), 93–97.

Patel, L. (2016). *Decolonizing educational research: From ownership to accountability*. New York, NY: Routledge.

Pearson, S. (2013). "The last bastion of colonialism": Appalachian settler colonialism and self-indigenization. *American Indian Culture and Research Journal, 37*(2), 165–184.

Petrone, R. (2015, November). Learning as a loss: Examining the affective dimensions to learning critical literacy. Paper presented at the NCTE Annual Convention, Minneapolis, MN.

Petrone, R. & Rink, N. with Speicher, C. (2020). From talking about to talking with: Integrating Native youth voices into teacher education via a repositioning pedagogy. *Harvard Educational Review, 90*(2), 243–268.

Petrone, R., Sarigianides, S.T., & Lewis, M.A. (2015). The youth lens: Analyzing adolescence/ts in literary texts. *Journal of Literacy Research, 46*(4), 506–533.

Poe, E.A. The Raven. Retrieved from https://www.poetryfoundation.org/poems/48860/the-raven

Red Elk, L. (2011). *Our blood remembers.* Kalispell, MT: Many Voices Press.

Said, E.W. (1978). *Orientalism.* New York City: Pantheon Books.

Sarigianides, S.T., Petrone, R., & Lewis, M.A. (2017). *Re-thinking the "adolescent" in adolescent literacy.* Chicago, IL: National Council for Teachers of English Press. Principles in Practice Series.

Schafft, K.A., & Jackson, A.Y. (Eds.). (2010). *Rural education for the twenty-first century.* State College, PA: Pennsylvania State University.

Scott, R. (2010). *Removing mountains: Extracting nature and identity in the Appalachian coalfields.* Minneapolis, MN: University of Minnesota Press.

Shotton, H.J., Lowe, S.C., & Waterman, S.J. (2013). *Beyond the asterisk: Understanding Native students in higher education.* Sterling, VA: Stylus.

Sierk, J. (2017). Redefining rurality: cosmopolitanism, whiteness, and the new Latino diaspora. *Discourse: Studies in the Cultural Politics of Education, 38*(3), 342–353.

Simmons, M., & Dei, G.J.S. (2012). Reframing anti-colonial theory for the diasporic context. *Postcolonial Directions in Education, 1*(1), 67–99.

Smith, A. (2016). Heteropatriarchy and the three pillars of white supremacy: Rethinking women of color organizing. In INCITE! Women of color against violence (Eds.), *Color of Violence: INCITE! Anthology* (pp. 66–73). Durham, NC: Duke University Press.

Smoker, M.L. Birthright. In D. Susag (Ed.), (2012) *Birthright: Born to poetry—A collection of Montana Indian poetry* (p. 98). Helena, MT: Montana Office of Public Instruction. Full text available http://opi.mt.gov/Portals/182/Page%20Files/Indian%20Education/Language%20Arts/Birthright%20Born%20to%20Poetry%20-%206-8%20and%20HS.pdf

Snell, A.H. (2001). *Grandmother's grandchild: My Crow Indian life.* Lincoln, NE: University of Nebraska Press.

Soul Fire Farm. (2018, May 15). Love notes: Farming while black, in sunshine and solidarity. *Soul Fire Farm.* Retrieved from http://www.soulfirefarm.org/farming-while-black-in-sunshine-and-solidarity/

Steele, C.M., & Aronson, J. (1995). Stereotype threat and the intellectual test performance of African Americans. *Journal of Personality & Social Psychology, 69*(5), 797–811.

References

Sue, D.W., Capodilupo, C.M., Torino, G.C., Bucceri, J.M., Holder, A.M.B., Nadal, K.L., & Esquilin, M. (2007). Racial microaggressions in everyday life: Implications for clinical practice. *American Psychologist, 62*(4), 271–286.

Sulzberger, A.G. (2011, November 13). Hispanics reviving faded towns on the plains. *The New York Times*. Retrieved from https://www.nytimes.com/2011/11/14/us/as-small-towns-wither-on-plains-hispanics-come-to-the-rescue.html

Supaman. (2015, September 4). *Supaman – Why*. [Video file]. Retrieved from https://www.youtube.com/watch?v=OiVU-W9VT7Q

Susag, D. (Ed.) (2013). *Birthright: Born to poetry—A collection of Montana Indian poetry*. Helena, MT: Montana Office of Public Instruction. Full text available http://opi.mt.gov/Portals/182/Page%20Files/Indian%20Education/Language%20Arts/Birthright%20Born%20to%20Poetry%20-%206-8%20and%20HS.pdf

Tabish, D. (2015, August, 19). CSKT prepares for historic acquisition of Kerr Dam. *Flathead Beacon*. Retrieved from https://flatheadbeacon.com/2015/08/19/cskt-prepares-for-historic-acquisition-of-kerr-dam/

Thieleman, K., & Cacciatore, J. (2014). Witness to suffering: Mindfulness and compassion fatigue among traumatic bereavement volunteers and professionals. *Social Work, 59*(1), 34–41.

Thomas, A.R., Lowe, B., Fulkerson, G., & Smith, P. (2011). *Critical rural theory: Structure, space, culture*. Lanham, MD: Lexington Books.

Thompson, D. (2011). "Somos del campo": Latino and Latina gardeners and farmers in two rural communities of Iowa—A community capitals framework approach. *Journal of Agriculture, Food Systems, and Community Development, 1*(3), 3–18.

Tieken, M.C. (2014) *Why rural schools matter*. Chapel Hill: University of North Carolina Press.

Tieken, M.C. (2017, March 24). There's a big part of rural America that everyone's ignoring. *The Washington Post*. Retrieved from https://www.washingtonpost.com/opinions/theres-a-big-part-of-rural-america-hat-everyones-ignoring/2017/03/24/d06d24d0-1010-11e7-ab07-07d9f521f6b5_story.html

Tschida, C.M., Ryan, C.L., & Ticknor, A.S. (2014). Building on windows and mirrors: Encouraging the disruption of single stories through children's literature. *Journal of Children's Literature, 40*(1), 28–39.

Tuck, E., & Yang, K.W. (2012). Decolonization is not a metaphor. *Decolonization: Indigeneity, Education and Society, 1*(1), 1–40.

United States Census Bureau. (2018, July 1). Quick facts Montana. Retrieved from https://www.census.gov/quickfacts/MT.

Valentin, A. (2018, October 19). Why rural communities of color are left behind: A call for intersectional demographic broadband data. *Public Knowledge*. Retrieved from https://www.publicknowledge.org/blog/why-rural-communities-of-color-are-left-behind-a-call-for-intersectional-demographic-broadband-data/

Vizenor, G. (2008). Aesthetics of survivance: Literary theory and practice. In G. Vizenor (Ed.), *Survivance: Narratives of Native presence* (pp. 1–24). Lincoln, NE: University of Nebraska Press.

Wallowitz, L. (Ed.). (2008). *Critical literacy as resistance: Teaching for social justice across the secondary curriculum.* New York: Peter Lang.

Williams, P.J. (2019, September 26). Stop getting married on plantations. *The Nation.* Retrieved from https://www.thenation.com/article/plantation-wedding-slavery/

Wolfe, P. (2006). Settler colonialism and the elimination of the Native. *Journal of Genocide Research, 8*(4), 387–409.

Wynhoff Olsen, A. (2017). Community Curricular Infusion: Cultivating the rural voice in literature, classrooms, and communities. Paper presented at the NCTE Annual Convention, St. Louis, MO.

Wynhoff Olsen, A. (2019). Tensions in ELA field experiences: Service learning in rural contexts. In Heidi Hallman, Kristen Pastore-Capuana, & Donna Pasternak (Eds.), *Methods into practice: New visions in teaching the English language arts methods class* (pp. 145–158). Lanham, MD: Rowman & Littlefield.

Wynhoff Olsen, A. (2020). Pearls, groves, and texts: Lessons learned by teaching ELA in rural places. In Ann Ellsworth (Ed.), *Cases on emotionally responsive teaching and mentoring* (pp. 259–271). Hershey, PA: IGI Global.

Wynhoff Olsen, A., & Branch, K. (with Hoffmann, A., Henwood, A., Kirby, H., Moos, C., Shannon, T., Strand, P., & Waterton, N.). (2018). Creating a team of teacher leaders in remote schools and local communities: The Yellowstone writing project's new pathway to leadership. National writing project resource from the building new pathways to leadership initiative. Retrieved from http://lead.nwp.org/knowledgebase/creating-a-team-of-teacher-leaders-in-remote-schools-and-local-communities-the-yellowstone-writing-projects-new-pathway-to-leadership/

Index

#MeToo movement, 88

abolitionist teaching, 83
access: to resources and amenities in the community, xiii, 93, 95, 97, 106, 119–20, 124, 128–36; to young adult literary representations of rurality, 31, 34, 86–87
activism, 7, 11, 50, 62, 91, 95, 98, 109, 119, 120, 134
academic aims and goals, 19, 25, 43–45, 51–55, 98, 125
acculturation, 88
addiction, 10, 69, 96
advocate/advocacy, 75–76, 93, 125, 134–35
agency, 89, 133
agrarian, 18, 59, 113
agriculture, 42, 67, 75, 77, 79, 81, 84, 97, 103, 110, 112
African Americans in rural America, 10, 42, 45, 103–6, 110–14, 116–17
alliances, 124–25
anti-colonial, 9, 48–50, 67
Appalachia, 92
Apsáalooke (Crow), 39, 41–43, 52, 65, 70, 109
Asterisk Nation, 107

BAM Fest, 113
Behrens, A., 8–9, 16–17, 19–20, 23, 27–28, 30–36, 38, 91–93, 119, 126–28, 131, 134
Black Belt, 110
Black Lives Matter, 44–45, 113
blackness, 112
boarding schools, 47, 53, 60, 65, 108
brain-drain, 6, 74, 75, 95, 96
Brayboy, B., 45–47, 109

censorship, 123
challenges (personal and professional) in teaching rural English Education, xi, xiii, 3, 11, 37, 78, 83, 91, 94, 97–98, 117, 119–36
colonization, 40, 45–52, 67, 71, 74, 96, 104, 106, 108. *See also* settler colonialism
Community Curricular Infusions (Wynhoff Olsen), 120–23, 125–26
community/ies: amenities, 83, 129; and curriculum, 20, 22, 24–25, 37–38, 73–98, 119–36; Native communities and community members, 45–51, 53, 55–56, 59, 62, 64, 66–67, 69–71, 107–9; racialization of rural, 101–17; rural communities, xi–xiv, 3–10,

155

16, 18, 22, 27, 35, 37, 40–42, 56, 62, 69–71, 73–98, 101–17, 119–36; visibility of, 107, 110–12, 115–16, 123, 127, 131
Confederated Salish Kootenai Tribes (CSKT), 17, 52, 58, 65, 86
Cree, 40, 52
critical conversations, 123
Critical Legal Studies, 45
critical literacy/ies, 7, 10, 21, 38, 43, 94, 98, 128
Critical Literature Pedagogy (Borsheim-Black et al), 20, 49
Critical Race Theory (CRT), 45
Critical Rural English Pedagogy (CREP), 6–11, 17, 36, 73, 76–78, 83, 90, 94, 119–22, 124–26, 129, 134
Critical Rural Perspective [CRP] (Behrens), 8, 17, 20–26, 30, 32–33, 35–38
Civil Rights movement, 45
critical theory, 20
Crone, S. B., 42
counternarratives, 8, 23, 67
cultural erasure, 5–6, 47, 68, 71, 106–7, 109, 115
Culturally Sustaining Pedagogy (Paris), 128
culture, xiv, 4–6, 20–21, 24–29, 35, 37, 46–47, 49, 51, 54–56, 58, 65, 67–71, 85, 93, 102–3, 106, 108–9, 113–17
curricular units, 17, 44, 94, 133

Dakota Access Pipeline (#NODAPL), 9, 44, 50–54, 58, 60–62, 64–65, 68, 109, 134
Dawes/General Allotment Act of 1887, 108
decolonization, 48–50
deficit-oriented discourse, 4–5, 11, 17, 20, 54, 58, 94
demographics: of rural communities, 4, 10, 18, 76, 85–86, 92, 94, 98, 101–3, 106, 107; of schools, 18, 42, 85, 98

de-weaponizing curriculum, 48–49, 54, 67
dialogic Pedagogy, 52, 60, 82–83, 96–97, 133–35
discourses of rurality, 4–8, 20–24, 29, 70, 93, 105, 113, 115, 116
displacement, 42, 76, 85, 91, 116
dissonance, 9, 68–69, 73–74, 76, 80, 90, 127, 134
Dorian, C., 9–10, 73–75, 83–93, 101, 119, 123, 126, 128, 131, 134, 155–56
Drum, K., 104–5

English: and literacy education, xi–xiv, 3–4, 7–11, 17, 24, 38, 45, 50, 91, 93–94, 96, 101, 103–4, 119–20, 122–23, 128, 131–34, 136; as school subject, xi–xiv, 3–4, 7–8, 10, 16, 18–19, 21, 24, 30, 38, 40, 43–44, 77–78, 82, 90–92, 94, 96, 98, 101, 113, 119–22, 126, 134; teachers, xi–xiv, 3–4, 9–11, 38, 73–74, 83, 85, 91, 93–98, 109, 117, 120–33, 136
essentialism, 92, 121
Essential Understandings for Montana Indians (MT), 51–52, 86
ethnocentrism, 44, 53–56

figurative language, 29
Flathead and Blackfeet Treaties of 1885, 59
Fort Laramie Treaty of 1851, 53, 59, 61
Fort Laramie Treaty of 1868, 53, 61
Freire, P., 7, 42–43, 50
Fryar, P. & M., 113

gender, 7, 17, 28, 43, 74, 87, 90, 95, 119
genocide, 44–45; cultural, 40, 104, 106–7, 109
Great Migration, 111
Great Retreat, 111

Herrera v. Wyoming, 109
heuristic, 20

home, xii–xiii, 58, 61, 69, 74, 77, 80, 82–83, 88, 91, 106, 113, 119–24, 130, 133, 135–36
homelands of Indigenous peoples, 17, 46, 51, 59, 61, 86, 88, 91, 108–9
homelessness, 95
homestead/ing, 29, 67, 70
hometown(s), 9, 16–17, 73, 75–76, 78, 101, 119
hooks, b., 42
Horner, M., 9–10, 39–45, 47–51, 53–55, 58, 61–62, 64, 66–69, 74, 91–93, 101, 119, 123, 126, 128, 131, 134, 156

identity/ies, 5–6, 19, 21–24, 38, 40–41, 44–46, 49, 51–52, 60, 65, 74, 86–88, 90–91, 101, 102, 104, 109, 115–16, 119, 129
ideology/ies, 7, 20, 22, 25, 33, 43, 45, 48–49, 51, 68, 112, 119–21, 126, 128
Indian Appropriations Act of 1851, 108
Indian Education for All (IEFA) (MT), 41, 47, 51, 86
Indian Removal Act of 1830, 108
indigeneity, 49, 67, 71, 109
indigenize/d, 5, 40, 45, 49–50
indigenous, 5, 9–10, 17, 40–53, 56–62, 64–71, 74, 76, 85–86, 88, 90–92, 96–98, 103–4, 106–10, 116–17, 137–39, 141–43
intersectionality, 3, 5, 49, 74, 86, 87, 90, 98, 101–3, 106, 109–10, 112, 114, 119–20, 136
isolation, 79, 84; professional isolation, 3–4, 85, 91, 131

Jim Crow, 111

land(s), 9, 10, 17, 41, 46–48, 50–54, 58–59, 75, 77, 91–93, 97, 106–10, 113–14, 120
landscape(s), 53, 83, 103, 107, 113–14, 125, 130

Latinx in Rural America, 10, 101–6, 114–17
Lawrence, D. T., 112
learning over time, 24, 120–21, 126–27, 134
LGBTQIA+ issues, 10, 74–75, 95
linguistic oppression, 108, 115
literary analysis, 20–22, 25–26, 33, 35, 38, 119
literary elements, 20–21, 33, 86
literary representations, 8, 21–23, 25–26, 33, 35, 38, 119, 122
Loewen, J., 43, 111

marginalization, 5–6, 31, 40, 45–47, 49–50, 71, 75, 91, 93, 95, 102, 106, 111, 115, 120, 134
mental health, 95–96, 129, 130
meta-moments (Petrone), 68–69
meta-knowledge, 21–23
Métis, 40, 52
metro-centrism, xii, 36
Missouri River, 61, 83–84
monoculture, 81
Montana, xi–xiv, 8, 16–19, 26–27, 29, 36–37, 39–42, 46, 50–59, 62, 65–70, 75–76, 79, 81, 83–88, 90, 92, 107, 111, 135
multiple exposures (Wynhoff Olsen), 126–27

National Congress of American Indians (NCAI), 107
National Council for Teachers of English, 131, 133
Native. *See* indigenous
Native (American) Studies, 53, 88
New Latino Diaspora (NLD) (Sierk), 114, 116

obstacles, 121
opportunity/ies, xi, 6, 10–11, 21, 24–25, 28, 36, 52, 67–68, 76–78, 80–83, 85–86, 89–90, 93, 95, 111, 119, 121–22, 127–31, 134

"the other" (Said), 115

Penniman, L., 113
Perma Red (novel; Earlin), 9, 74, 86–90
personal narrative, 8, 25–26, 36–37
Petrone, R., xii, 156–57
Piikani (Blackfeet), xiv, 59, 85
place: culture, identity and, 27, 86–87, 93, 110, 117; gender and, 90, 119; imagination and sense of, 5, 17, 20, 23–24, 78, 82; indigeneity, Indigenous peoples and, 40, 45, 47–50, 56, 62, 66–71, 108; race/ism, racialization and, 9, 67, 86–88, 90, 93, 103–4, 110–17, 119, 128; reading and writing, 10–25, 29–32, 35, 38, 41, 49, 78–81; representation and, 21–22, 77, 110; reputation and, 86–87, 89, 128; rural(ity) and, 4–9, 20–24, 31–32, 35, 38, 40, 48, 60, 64, 67–71, 75–76, 83, 87–88, 93–94, 97, 103–4, 106–7, 110, 113–17, 119–21, 123, 126; sex(uality) and, 86–87, 89–90; space and, 112, 86–87, 89–90, 93–94, 103, 106, 112; urban(ity) and, 22, 35, 108, 110
Place-Based Pedagogy, 9, 19, 39–72, 77–83, 103
place-conscious pedagogy, 7–8, 21–23, 120
plains regions, 41, 70, 76, 107
poetry, 9, 25, 29, 50, 52–52, 65, 73, 77–78, 80–82, 88
porous boundaries (Cuervo), 127
positionality/ies, 21, 66, 75, 127–28
positioning, 46, 82, 120
postcolonialism, 85
poverty, 4, 10, 74–75, 85, 97
power, 5, 7–9, 20, 23–24, 46–49, 52, 107, 119, 121
powwow, 67, 70
privacy, xiii, 96
professional development, xiii, 11, 129–31, 133

professional networks, xiii, 3, 129–34

race/ism, 5, 7, 10, 17, 42–47, 65, 68, 74, 86–87, 90, 92, 98, 101–6, 110–14, 117, 119–20, 122, 128
racial literacy, 43–44
racial positionality, 102
racial silencing, 74, 86, 90, 93
Reierson, L., 9–10, 73–83, 91–94, 119, 126–28, 131, 134, 157
relationships, xi, 20, 22, 39–40, 48, 51, 70, 75, 77, 84, 86–89, 95, 109, 113–14, 120–23, 125–29
representations: of African Americans in criminal justice system, 110–11; of Indigenous peoples, 45, 48–49, 56–58, 66; of Latinx community members, 115; of rurality, 4–8, 21–23, 25–30, 32–33, 35–36, 38, 40, 77, 93–94, 105–6, 110, 119, 121
reputation(s), 10, 74, 84–87, 89–90, 119, 128
reservation, 5, 10, 40, 42, 50–54, 69, 86, 92, 97, 104, 107–8; Apsáalooke (Crow), 42; Blackfeet, xiv; Flathead, 53, 58–59, 74, 86, 89, 138; Fort Peck Indian, 88; Little Elk, 58–59; Rocky Boy Indian, 85; Standing Rock Lakota, 60–63, 66, 68, 109; Tongue River, 76
Rink, N. xiv
Rocky Mountains, 41, 85, 107
Román-Odio, C., 116
rural, xi–xiv, 3–11, 16–18, 20–28, 30–42, 45, 48, 50–51, 56, 58–62, 64, 67–71, 73–78, 82–87, 90–98, 101–17, 119–24, 126–36; as a social construct, 7, 20–23, 70, 92, 94, 102–3, 107, 119, 127–28
rurality/ies, xi–xii, 3–11, 17, 20–24, 27–31, 33, 36–41, 50, 59–61, 64, 67–71, 73–74, 77, 82, 84, 87–88, 90–95, 97–98, 101–10, 112–17, 119–21, 124, 126, 134

Rust Belt, 104

scaffolding, 25, 33
secondary trauma, 130
segregation, 42, 65, 93, 104, 108, 112
self-care, 11, 129–31
sexuality, 10, 43, 74, 86–87, 90
setting, 6, 21–22, 25–26, 30–32, 34–35, 86, 89, 90, 131
settler colonialism, 9–10, 40, 42, 47–50, 58, 59, 67–70, 76, 85, 103–4, 108–9, 115, 119, 125. *See also* colonization
single story (Adichie), 5, 23, 26, 28, 33, 56, 92, 93, 104
"slut shaming," 10, 74, 86–87
social justice, 4, 7–8, 48, 84, 93, 104, 112, 134–36
sovereignty: food sovereignty, 97–98; self-determination, 40, 46, 97; tribal sovereignty, 9, 40, 46, 48–52, 88, 98, 109
South, the, 105, 110–13
stereotypes: of indigenous peoples, 45–46, 67; of rural, 4–6, 17, 21–23, 25–28, 76–77
stereotype threat, 5–6, 115
suburban, xiii–xiv, 4, 93, 111, 123, 131, 133, 135
sundown towns (Loewen), 42–43, 111–12
surveillance, 127, 130
survivance (Vizenor), 48, 109

teacher housing, 135–36
teacher status, 27, 74, 84, 97, 120, 126–28

tension(s): labor-related, 82, 125, 124; pedagogical, 9, 82, 96; social, 97, 98; textual, 9, 58
textual analysis, 10, 21–22, 25, 86
textual consumption, 7, 9
textual distribution, 7, 10, 119
textual identity, 22–23
textual production, 7, 9, 10, 20, 22, 29, 119
Treaties of Fort Laramie 1851 and 1868, 53, 59, 61
TribalCrit Theory (Brayboy), 45–50
tribal nation(s), 39, 45, 48, 50–59, 61, 63–66, 71, 85, 91–92, 107–9, 137, 139, 141–43
Trump, D. J., 102
Tsétsehéstahese (Northern Cheyenne), 76
Tuck, E. & Yang, W., 50

urban, xii–xiv, 4, 6, 17, 21–23, 31, 35, 75, 93, 104, 106–8, 110–12, 123, 131, 134–35

water protectors, 61–62, 66, 70, 109
whiteness, 101–4, 123
white supremacy, 46, 49, 93, 104, 110, 116
whitewashing, 102
wobble (Fecho), 127, 134
workload/work demands, xi–xiv, 85, 128, 130, 135
Wynhoff Olsen, A., xi, 120, 126, 131

young adult literature, 20, 24–26, 30–31, 122
youth lens (Petrone), 20, 86

About the Authors

Raised in a small town in Eastern Arizona, **Alli Behrens** was drawn to teaching while attending college at Northern Arizona University, and she graduated with her bachelor's degree in English Education with the intention of teaching in a rural community. Shortly after marrying her husband Joe, the two moved to Southwestern Montana where Alli began her career teaching 6-12 English in a rural school. After teaching for several years, she completed her Library Media Certificate and master's degree in English at Montana State University. Alli's teaching experiences combined with her graduate school research instilled in her a passion for addressing the educational inequities faced by rural teachers and students. Because of this, Alli strives to utilize place-based curriculum in her classroom to provide both windows and mirrors for her students, helping them gain an appreciation for those in the world outside of their community while also recognizing their own inherent value and importance as rural people. Outside of the classroom, Alli spends her time raising her two wild little girls, hiking in the mountains, and reading any book she can. She has presented her work at the Montana Educators' Conference, National Council of Teachers of English Annual Convention, and the International Symposium for Innovation in Rural Education. She is currently residing and teaching in Eastern Oregon.

Catherine Dorian was raised in both central Massachusetts and Upstate New York in the Adirondacks. A need to escape the east coast took her to Montana, where she earned a B.A. in English Education and a minor in Native American Studies from Montana State University. During her undergrad, Catherine spent her summers living and learning on both the Northern Cheyenne and Blackfeet reservations. From 2012 to 2016, Catherine taught English in Fort Benton, Montana, where she realized the excitement and stimulation that a rural setting may offer. Teaching rural also compelled her to find community with other professionals, and she delivered two presentations at the Montana Educators Association Annual Conference and three presentations at the National Council of Teachers of English Annual Convention. Her article, "Reputation and Rurality: Using a Montana-Authored Text to Talk About Agency and Language in the Secondary English Classroom" was published in the *Montana English Journal* in the Spring of 2019. Catherine has since relocated back to the northeast and is teaching high school English in Brattleboro, VT. An introvert, she finds comfort in books, freedom in hiking, joy in her yoga practice, and relief in writing. Catherine is currently a degree candidate in the MLA program in Creative Writing and Literature at Harvard University; most of her pieces converge in their commentary on living in rural spaces, a setting for which she holds preference. Some of her writing can be found on writingrural.com.

Melissa Horner (Métis/Anishinaabe) grew up in Montana and revels in opportunities to practice archery, beadweave, read, hunt, and hike with her dog Koy, all of which shape the cultural and personal experiences that continuously inform her thinking, writing, research, teaching, and creativity. After teaching in rural Montana, Melissa transitioned to a Ph.D. program in Sociology at the University of Missouri. Her research interests cohere around exploring how tribal nations and Native individuals interrupt and heal the effects of intergenerational historical trauma caused by past and present settler colonization. Melissa pursues her research and doctoral degree as a Health Policy Research scholar for the Robert Wood Johnson Foundation. She has presented her work at the National Council for Teachers of English Annual Convention, the Montana Education Association Annual Conference, Montana Annual Indian Education for All Best Practices Conference, and as part of the National Native American Heritage Month at the University of Missouri. One of Melissa's recent publications, "Resistance, Reception, Race, and Rurality: Teaching Non-canonical Texts in a White, Conservative Montana Context," can be found in Mollie Blackburn's *Adventurous Thinking: Students' Rights to Read and Write* (National Council for Teachers of English, 2019).

Dr. Robert Petrone is an associate professor of Literacy/English Education and Critical Youth Studies at the University of Missouri where he coordinates the Language & Literacies for Social Transformation doctoral program and is co-founder of the Missouri Language & Literacies Center. Prior to Mizzou, Robert was faculty at Montana State University and the University of Nebraska-Lincoln, earned graduate degrees in English at Northern Arizona University and Michigan State University, and taught middle and high school English in New York and Colorado. As an educational researcher, his work moves across several domains, including: examining youth cultural practices (e.g., skateboarding), developing curricula with high school English teachers to facilitate critical (media) literacy, analyzing young adult literature through a "youth lens," and integrating high school students into teacher education as curricular consultants and experts by way of a "repositioning pedagogy." In 2018, he established, alongside several community members, a literacy center in the rural Ruboni Village in the Republic of Uganda. In 2019, he received a Spencer Foundation Grant to conduct research in collaboration with an alternative high school on a Native American reservation. His work has been published in a wide range of educational journals, including *Harvard Educational Review*, *English Teaching: Practice & Critique*, *Teaching and Teacher Education*, and *Journal of Literacy Research*. He is also co-author (along with Drs. Sophia Sarigianides and Mark A. Lewis) of the book *Re-thinking the "Adolescent" in Adolescent Literacy* (National Council for Teachers of English, 2017). Robert identifies as a white, cisgender male who grew up in and around New York City amid parental disability—all of which has shaped his personal and cultural experiences and informs (and limits) his research, teaching, writing, and living. Feel free to reach out to him at petroner@missouri.edu.

Liz Reierson, the daughter of an extension agent and a cattle rancher, was born and raised in rural southeastern Montana. Her parents' love and dedication to their community has inspired her advocacy for rural communities and people. After graduating with her B.A. degree in English Education from Montana State University-Bozeman (MSU), Liz launched her career as a rural educator teaching English and Spanish in grades 9–12 in a small school. In 2015, she married her husband Phil and returned to southeastern Montana where she continues to teach English and Spanish while sharing her passion for the local community with her students. Away from the classroom, Liz and her husband raise their two kids and cattle in Rosebud, Montana. Liz achieved her Masters in English from MSU in 2020 and continues to find ways to bring the local community into the classroom. She has presented her work at the Montana Educators Conference, National Council of Teachers of English Annual Convention, and the International Symposium for Innovation in Rural Education.

Dr. Allison Wynhoff Olsen is an associate professor of English Education at Montana State University and Director of the Yellowstone Writing Project. She earned her Ph.D. in teaching and learning from the Ohio State University and taught high school English in rural Minnesota. Using her teaching foundation, Allison is a scholar invested in how we use language, socially and relationally; she operates from a qualitative methodology and is influenced by sociocultural theories of learning. Allison's research aims to better understand how teachers and students co-construct knowledge, and she is invested in creating curricular opportunities that promote dignity, offer dialogic conversation, and promote place-conscious pedagogies. She is interested in argumentative writing; student writing development over time; and rural English teaching, with a focus on both experiences of rural English teachers and pre-service teacher preparations. Thus far, her scholarship emphasizes the social and relational processes within the teaching and learning of argumentative writing, as well as tracings of talk and text in written arguments. Her work appears in co-authored books such as *Teaching and Learning Argumentative Writing in High School English Language Arts Classrooms* (Routledge, 2015) and *Dialogic Literary Argumentation in High School English Language Arts Classrooms* (Routledge, 2020) and peer-reviewed journals such as *Learning, Culture, and Social Interaction*; *Written Communication*; the *Journal of Adolescent and Adult Literacy*; and *Research in the Teaching of English*. Her rural scholarship examines teachers' professional practices, teachers' emotional strain, and pre-service teacher preparations for rural contexts. This work appears in *The Rural Educator*, book chapters, and a National Writing Project report, as well as numerous conference presentations. With her colleague Dr. Jennifer VanDerHeide, Allison is conceptualizing and developing curricular moves for a particular kind of argument, a *listening argument*. Allison is also leading two initiatives through the Yellowstone Writing Project: a teacher study group examining the works and archive of MT author, Ivan Doig, and a development of how silent films amplify listening and promote more nuanced cultural understanding.

www.ingramcontent.com/pod-product-compliance
Lightning Source LLC
Chambersburg PA
CBHW022013300426
44117CB00005B/175